"Ex-homicide cop Don DuPay is the real deal. Why, if you didn't know better, you might find a resemblance or two between him and the fictional tough-guy private eye in his new novel *Frank's Revenge: Albina After Dark.*"
—Phil Stanford,
author of *Rose City Vice: Portland in the 70s*

"Frank's Revenge: Albina After Dark is a great read. Don DuPay brings 1970s Portland to life and populates it with characters as unique and idiosyncratic as the city itself. A natural storyteller, DuPay not only makes the long-gone decades of Portland live again, he weaves a gripping detective story that will have you on the edge of your seat from beginning to end!"
—JD Chandler,
author of *Murder and Scandal in Prohibition Portland*

"DuPay's bare-knuckle prose sends readers reeling into gritty 1970s Portland and the payback is solid."
—JB Fisher,
author of *Echo of Distant Water and Portland on the Take*

"Don DuPay's all-too-real street prose captures the hard truths of 1970s Portland, a city teeming with corruption, fear, and, if you look hard enough, courage. His memorable debut novel puts the Rose City on the noir map."
—Doug Perry,
author of *Eliot Ness: The Rise and Fall of an American Hero*

"What could be finer than to be in Albina with Don Dupay and his fictional character Frank - his doppelgänger who uncovers the real underbelly of Portland in a breakthrough novel!"
—Kathy Smith,
former KGW anchorwoman

DuPay writes a vintage noir crime story that sheds light on the ugly racism and crookedness of the Portland Police Bureau in the mid-1970s. Long ago fired from the PPB, Frank is now working private investigations when he's hired to find a serial killer who's stalking the black community in North Portland. Raw and dark, with lots of politically incorrect language, DuPay's story is engaging with interesting characters and the tiniest hope of a happy ending.

~Dianah Hughley, *Powell's Books*

Set in Portland in 1975, Frank's Revenge: Albina After Dark is a short novel about an ex-cop working a freelance case for cash amid the corruption and racism of his former brothers. Down on his luck, Frank has been working as a private investigator repossessing cars from big shots in Portland's West Hills and Lake Oswego. Frank begins most days in the Lotus Hotel, where he has a Bloody Mary served by Midge, the longtime barmaid and friend to regulars. As Frank sorts bills at the bar, he's approached by a beautiful young black woman named Theda, whose brother was shot to death in the Albina neighborhood by a killer the neighborhood has dubbed Batman. DuPay ("Behind the Badge in River City: A Portland Police Memoir") sloshes around in Portland's gritty history and recalls well his days spent in its bars and after-hours joints. DuPay's novel serves its purpose well: acting as a hook where the author can hang his memories of working as a police officer and police detective from 1961-1978.

~*The Portland Tribune Newspaper*

FRANK'S REVENGE
Albina After Dark

FRANK'S REVENGE
REVENGE
Albina After Dark

Don DuPay

OREGON
GREYSTONE
PRESS

Portland, Oregon

First Edition: 2019

ISBN: 978-0-578-22095-6

Cover photograph: *Lotus Cardroom II* © Scott Allen Tice
scottaticephoto.com

Set in Optima and Bembo MT Pro

I dedicate my debut novel to my wife and editor, Theresa, without whom this book would merely be crumpled paper on the kitchen floor.

"Experience is simply the name we give our mistakes."
—Oscar Wilde

Contents

Preface

I ALWAYS SAW the young woman in distress walking hurriedly along SW Fourth Avenue in downtown Portland, glancing at her wristwatch and fearing she was late for an appointment. I thought perhaps she was trying to get to the pawnshop before it closed to retrieve her wedding ring. I never knew who she was or exactly where she was going, but I knew someday she would become part of a story I would write.

Now the young woman comes alive in *Frank's Revenge: Albina after Dark*. She is part and parcel of the lost tenderloin district that was SW Third and Fourth Avenue from Burnside to SW Jefferson in the 1960's. Anchored by the Lotus bar and hotel and The Old Glory, along with the nefarious Hamilton Hotel, the tenderloin was a place populated by a myriad of Damon Runyon characters—street hookers, drunken transients, lost souls and derelict Indians from nearby Warm Springs reservation.

The Lotus Hotel was an important part of the tenderloin, too, as I came to experience it. Home of cheap rooms rented by the hour handily just up the stairs from the street level bar, it was a magnet. Now room #10 at the Lotus, the first room past the old desk clerks office, is both office and living quarters for PI Frank McAllister, a composite of a lot of middle age ex-cops worn out from trying to make the system work, and having failed, try to salvage a meaningful existence of what's left of life.

Having actually worked the old tenderloin both as a uniformed officer and as a Vice cop I now lament its disappearance—with its rich history of early Portland, and the characters whose existence created the very flavor of the area. I miss the blue police call-box that stood across the street from the Lotus, and the numerous "unlicensed drinking establishments," called at various times, "speakeasies," or "after-hours joints," or even "blind pigs." I miss the cat and mouse, catch-me-if-you-can games old cops and robbers played with each other, sometimes winning, sometimes losing.

With *Frank's Revenge: Albina after Dark* I hope to return the reader to yesteryear to immerse them in the flavor, the foggy nights and the intrigue of the glittering streets of the disappearing tenderloin. The Old Glory, originally located on First and Main Street is torn down now, but I remember its dimensions well and its unpleasant smell perfectly. The Lotus and the many after-hours joints that were an important part of Portland's history are gone as well, never to return. This is the cost of progress, the loss of our cities history. But maybe some parts of it can be saved.

Let's read along Dear Reader, and see how Frank, the young woman I call Theda, and old Indian Charlie make out in the no-longer-land of the old tenderloin of old Portland, combating the forces of corruption that existed right out in the open among the men in the uniform.

Prologue; Waiting in the Dark

*T*HE NIGHT IS *still—the kind of stillness that comes after four in the morning and blankets the neighborhood with a palpable thickness. It's misting, not raining but misting, enough so the driver of the Black '69 Cadillac parked on North Commercial must intermittently clear his view using the windshield wipers. The man sitting at the wheel is dressed in black pants, black turtleneck, and a black jacket. Over his head is a ski-mask pulled down, covering the skin of his neck. The hood of his jacket conceals his face. On the seat beside him is a blue steel Smith and Wesson .38 special loaded with six rounds. It has a four inch barrel and a blade front sight; the man's hands are covered with tight fitting black leather gloves. The grain of the leather is visible, and glimmers in the dim light. The engine is running but makes almost no sound. The ninja figure watches a particular house at the end of the street. It's boarded up and abandoned like most of the houses on the block. A For Rent sign hangs askew on the front porch, and only three or four of the houses are occupied. Several have been destroyed by fire and closed up by the city. The derelict cement front steps of some of the homes have fallen apart and crumbled. The loose sections become convenient chunks of concrete for breaking windows in abandoned cars and houses. The boarded up houses and junker cars are all that remains of a once thriving Portland community.*

The Ninja in the Cadillac is watching something as it moves forward unsteadily. People walk up the driveway and disappear behind the back of a corner house. Others leave, get into their cars and drive away. The Ninja is watching a black only after-hours club and the people who wander in and wander out. He puts the Cadillac in gear and creeps silently forward with the lights off. A lone figure appears, walking slowly down the driveway, towards the street, unsteady in gait and demeanor. Finding the sidewalk the person stumbles forward, heading toward the corner. The Cadillac glides to a stop directly alongside what appears to be a young man, and the passenger door opens.

"Gimme yer fuckin' money!" the Ninja demands in a terse whisper.

The blue steel revolver clicks ominously as the hammer is pulled back. The young man turns and responds.

"Screw you, mutherfucker!"

He turns to run, but can only lurch on unsteady feet toward the corner. The ninja in black opens the driver's door, steps out and calmly lowers both arms to the top of the door to steady his hand. He aims at the man and fires three shots in rapid succession—the explosions split the four a.m. quiet. Propelled forward by the force of three .38 slugs in his back the man crumples to the sidewalk, falling on his knees first and then his face. His body seizes, quivers, struggling to breathe, fighting to hang on, but the man is dying. The shooter jogs forward, reaches down, and turns the man over on his back, careful not to bloody his gloves. He finds no exit wounds. Satisfied the slugs are still in the man's back and he's dead, the shooter turns his pockets inside out and removes a fine Italian wallet. He pulls out the legal tender and tosses the leather wallet into the middle of the street. Returning to his car, he slips into the driver's seat, reaching over and closing the passenger door. He puts the car in gear, moves silently away, and runs over the dead man's once fine wallet.

"Stupid fuckin' nig-nog!" he mutters under his breath.

The Cadillac turns the first corner and is lost in the infinite Albina darkness. The dead man lies on his back, motionless. A fine mist covers his beard stubble and gathers on the fine hairs of his eyebrows; his glittering dark eyes are open, staring at a darkness he can no longer perceive. His face is illuminated only by the street lamp on the corner; a light that sputters for a few seconds and then goes out.

The Albina night sees a black man in his middle thirties. His mouth is open and shows a gold front tooth. The lips are parted and blood has pooled darkly in his mouth and throat. His face is scratched from the sidewalk where it scraped his cheeks and his nose is broken, also a result of the fall. The black hair is short and has been secured in tight braids, with the ends crimped with small sections of aluminum foil. The dark clothing is shabby. Blue jeans with patches cover holes on the knees. A black sport jacket with the sleeves pushed up to the elbows has a designer label but is long past its prime, an older fashion, no longer in style.

Who will find this man's body as dawn chases away the inky darkness? Perhaps a child on their way to school, or a person headed to the nearest bus stop for work? Or maybe the body will be found by the garbage collector or a street cleaner, or a taxi driver. Or maybe someone will walk by and simply do nothing at all. In time, the police will be called and will make a chalk outline on the sidewalk, take photographs, and make notes in their field notebooks. They will talk to anyone in the neighborhood who answers the door. They will note that no one heard any shots or has any idea who the deceased man is. The officers will call the morgue and two men will arrive from the coroner's office. The men will maneuver the body into a black zip-up bag and slide it into the van—the same van the officers sometimes call "the meat wagon." The blood on the sidewalk will remain, untouched. Perhaps the rain will wash it away before too many people see it and wonder what happened; perhaps not. This is Albina after all and no one really cares in Albina, in 1975.

Sidewalks and Neon Signs

ANYONE WATCHING HER would say she was showing a lot of cleavage. Her boobs were pushing up and out of a low-cut pink sweater, bouncing rhythmically as she hurried along Third Avenue. From the back, her form fitting, crotch-tight blue jeans showed every inch of her abbreviated panty line. She glanced at the watch on her wrist. The time read 5:20 P.M., so she quickened her step. She knew it was late and hoped her watch was wrong. She was getting closer, intent on catching him as he left his office.

Frank stood in front of the old 1906 Lotus hotel. With crumbling masonry and pigeons collecting on the upstairs window ledges, the Lotus was an edifice of old Portland. If you were down on your luck, the Lotus was one of the cheapest places in town to rent in the tenderloin district. Frank rented room number ten, on the second floor. The room was large enough for the oak desk he'd purchased from Multnomah County when they sold the old courthouse furniture. On his desk sat a dusty black Rolodex and an old Royal manual typewriter that he used regularly. A dented, grey file cabinet sat next to the desk—all the furniture was shabby but still useful. He managed to fit an older leather couch on the far wall behind the desk. He was comfortable with his office equipment. Like Frank, it was past its prime, but still reliable and strong.

Fishing around in his pockets Frank found his old Zippo and fired up a Marlboro long. He coughed, remembering his promise to quit. He stood on the avenue, gathering his thoughts, pulling on the cigarette deeply and scanning the street. He considered whether he should go back in and have a drink or jay walk across the street and see if George was open in the basement of the Blind Pig. Frank was surprised when he felt a tentative tugging at his sleeve.

"Are you Frank McAllister?" the woman asked. She looked frantic and out of breath.

"Who wants to know, honey?"

He took another drag on his cigarette and exhaled directly in her face, slightly annoyed at being accosted on the street by a woman he didn't know. He glanced down with appraising yet wary eyes. She was cute and curvy, hair medium length in a soft Jerry Curl, with large luminescent amber eyes. He hoped she would turn around so he could get a look at her butt, but she just stood there looking up at him, her face an alluring question mark of uncertainty.

"I'm Theda. I've left you three phone messages, but you don't answer. I need to talk with you. It's about my brother Jojo." Frank was reluctant to engage the woman, but since she was pretty and smelled good he decided for once not to be rude.

"My office hours are from ten A.M. to five P.M. and now it's exactly five twenty two P.M. Come back tomorrow at the proper time, and we can talk." Frank turned to leave, but stopped when she spoke again, touching his arm briefly.

"My brother was murdered and I heard you used to be a *real* police detective!"

"Then call a cop!" Frank replied, more than a little exasperated, hoping he could kiss her off and take a nap on his couch after another quick drink.

"No! You have to help! The city cops won't talk to me anymore. You know how they are!" She tugged at his sleeve again with a new sense of urgency.

"I'll buy you a drink?" she offered hopefully.

Frank turned back to her and looked her right in the eyes. She seemed afraid and that worried him. She was holding back tears and might become distraught, possibly even make a scene.

"Okay, Theda...that is your name, right?"

"Yeah. Can I buy you a drink?"

"Nah, no need; I have a tab here. Why don't we go inside?"

Frank steered the pretty woman to his favorite booth, his hand pressed lightly to the middle of her back. The booth was within shouting range of the bartender and only a few steps from the men's room. The counter seats were crammed with the after work crowd making noise and having fun. A fat businessman in a pale blue, ill-fitting leisure suit pontificated loudly about politics, the "modern woman" and his great new job. He announced he was going to buy everyone drinks once he got his first paycheck. His girlfriend seemed embarrassed, she motioned for him to sit down, pulling on his sleeve, but he ignored her, laughing and smiling and acting like a big shot. Frank brushed past the man as he approached the bar.

"Hey Pagan!" Frank yelled over the din of the bar.

Marty looked up from the sink where he was washing shot glasses. He had told Frank the story of how his father moved the family from Puerto Rico to an Irish neighborhood in New York and changed his name from Martinique Pagan to Marty Griffin. His father figured if they changed their Puerto Rican names, the family could fit in better, despite the fact they were brown and didn't resemble any Irish folks in town.

"Ya know my name is Griffin?" Marty shot back.

"Is that right?"

"I'm Irish!" Marty said laughing. "I *feel* Irish, anyway," he muttered, looking away.

"I'll have my regular" said Frank, smiling and giving a friendly nod.

"Theda here will have—what will you have Miss Theda?"

"I'll have a Mimosa," Theda said, smiling and beginning to relax.

Theda was eager to get the conversation going now that she had Frank's full attention. She moved closer to the table sticking her chest out and rummaging in her purse. Marty showed up with the drinks, sliding them across the counter, watching Frank as he took a sip. Frank quietly observed Theda with wary eyes, and then turned back to Marty.

"Can you add a little more sweet Vermouth?" he asked. Marty shrugged, pulling his comically forlorn eyes away from Theda's full breasts.

"Sure, Frank. No problem."

"What's a Mimosa, Theda?" Frank asked.

"Orange juice and champagne—girlie stuff."

A sneer of annoyance turned slowly to a smile as Frank watched Theda take dainty sips from her Mimosa, careful not to muss her lip gloss. She gazed over the top of her glass at Frank, sizing him up with flirtatious eyes. Marty reappeared with the Manhattan, sliding it over to Frank.

"Perfect. Thanks, old man."

"Sure, thing Frank."

"Now, Miss Theda, who told you where to find me?"

"Some of the older guys—in the life—ya know, the OG's? They said you might be the right person who could help. They said you were an ex-detective with a grudge, whatever *that* means."

"Did they tell you I don't work for free—even if I *do* agree to help ya?"

"I can pay—some. The OG's will help, too. They don't like cops much. Most black folks don't in case ya didn't notice."

"Okay, look, we need to get a few things straight, first. Back in the day, I was a street cop for ten years working the ghetto in the North End. I was promoted to detective but got into a little trouble before I got my detective badge. Then I was canned. I'm not a cop anymore."

"Whaja do wrong? And, Can I call you Frank?"

"Long story," Frank replied, sipping his drink, leaving a few drops in the glass.

"I'm listening?"

"Yeah, Frank's my name. My friends just call me Mac. But I don't *have* any!" Frank chuckled at his own joke. Theda, unimpressed, said nothing, eyebrows raised.

"So, what went wrong, Frank?"

"Nothing—in fact I did the world a favor. His name was Jesus Vahto, a Mexican gangster, dope dealer, pimp, hater of women and armed robber when he ran outa money. I arrested him a dozen times over the years I worked the Albina ghetto. He went to the pen once for three years for pistol whipping an elderly clerk during a drugstore robbery. The old guy was beat-up pretty bad and wound up in the hospital for three weeks."

"Did the clerk live?"

"Yeah, sure, he lived, but my fuckin' Sergeant, that asshole Cunningham showed up at the sentencing. He told the judge that Vahto had seen a tough life and after all, he hadn't killed anyone and by golly he deserved a second chance."

"Second chances are important."

"Yeah, they are, but Vahto was a scumbag. And Cunningham was a prick. He shoulda gone to jail *with* Vahto! Never could figure out what the connection was, unless the sergeant was a john for one of his whores or sniffin' some of his dope. I think the judge gave Vahto three instead of the five he shoulda got."

"Did he come back to the neighborhood?"

"Oh yeah. You know the score. When Vahto got outa the joint he came right back and within a week I was gettin' calls about him. He was still beatin' up young girls tryin' to get'em hooked on coke or heroin so he could turn em' out."

"I know the score, I've seen more than my share of ruined girls' cause of some pimp."

"Yep, he was a stinkin' piece of shit, that fucker! I tried to get him bitched back to the joint but it never worked thanks to Cunningham. But Cunningham wasn't the only one stickin' his nose in it. It coulda' been that fucker Lt. Drake, too. Or maybe someone else."

"Who's Drake?"

"Drake and Cunningham were buddies and as crooked as they come. Drake was the lieutenant and a racist sack-a-shit. So it never made any sense why they were in Vahto's corner unless they were in business together." Frank waved his now almost empty glass at Marty.

"Another round," he mouthed quietly." Marty nodded and reached up for the Vermouth bottle.

"Yeah, they were in the dope business with Vahto, alright. It's obvious they were!"

"Dope is everywhere."

"Yeah, well, my dream finally came true."

"What was that?"

"I got a call one night on a knife fight in the six hundred block of Russell. When I pull up I see Vahto bleeding on the sidewalk. I kneel down to take a look and can see he's been stabbed in the chest and neck, deep wounds, too. Blood everywhere, running into the mossy cracks of the sidewalk, turning the moss purple under my flashlight. His glassy eyes look up at me…"

"What happened next?"

"He just laid there, lookin' up at me. 'Call me a am-bu-lance, Frank? he begged."

"That's so sad."

"It's too late, man. You're already dead."

"What? Is that what you told him?"

"Yeah, I wasn't gonna lie to him. I shook my head at him. I'd busted him so many times he remembered my name! No, I wasn't gonna lie to him. I walked back to the car and put in a call for the coroner. I knew he'd be dead before the meat wagon arrived—saved the ambulance a god-damned trip."

"Did you find the guy who stabbed him?"

"Nah. Didn't look. Didn't care. It was probably a dope deal gone wrong, anyway. Whoever the guy was, he did the world a favor. I'd a probably let him go and thanked him, if I ever came across him." Frank paused, finished the rest of his Manhattan and then looked at Theda with an expression of fatigue and apathy, like a worn out soldier.

"I got kicked out and fired for "allowing" this useless piece of crap to die on the sidewalk. I didn't "allow" him to die. He was dying and didn't have two minutes left. He did the world a favor, when he got cut that night. Cunningham found out though, and fired me for "failing to provide necessary aid" as he put it. And Lt. Drake backed him up. They were pissed that he died, so I *know* they were dirty, otherwise why would they care? They didn't give a damn about Vahto personally; it was just business to them. Their partner was dead. They lost *money* on him! I was so disgusted with the police after that, that I didn't give a shit about leaving. I was beating my head against a wall in Albina. Nothing I ever did made a difference, anyway."

"I'm sure you helped *some* people. What happened after they got rid of you?"

"I took several months off living off the money I'd accumulated in what woulda been my pension fund. It took me a while to decide what to do next. I thought I'd promote *myself* to detective—a private detective, a pay for service kinda thing. That's me now. Pay for service. Ya know Theda, pay for service?"

Frank sneered, laughing cynically, and waited for her reaction. His sarcasm was more blatant than he had intended, but Theda just nodded and finished her Mimosa ignoring the innuendo, distracted and preoccupied with her own thoughts.

"Ya gonna help me find the guy who shot my brother JoJo three times in the back—leavin' him dead on the street like an animal?" Her tone was impatient, so she softened it with a bitter smile.

"I'm gonna need a retainer, money up front. I gotta survive, you know? I'll start with $5000. How's that?" Frank thought he'd test the water trying for a big retainer, but Theda responded like he expected. She stood up, opened her purse and threw down a ten dollar bill.

"I'll buy my own fuckin' drinks. You don't give a shit my brother was murdered. You don't give a fuck. Why would you? You're white! And you're just like—like *everyone* else! All you care about is *yourself!*" She sputtered looking for more dirty words to call Frank.

"And—and you're just another white asshole!" she spat out in conclusion.

"Come on, honey, I'm a tired old man. We've all got a story, even you."

"Where ya think I'm gonna get five g's?" Frank shrugged and joined Marty watching Theda as she stomped out of the Lotus, tossing her leather purse over her shoulder and swinging her hips.

"Nice butt," Marty said, conspiratorially. Frank agreed with a philosophical nod of his head.

"Pretty too, and young," he mumbled into his drink.

A Bloody Mary and a Bowl of Soup

THE PHONE RANG at exactly 10:07 A.M. Frank rolled over on the couch and waited for the answering machine to pick up. He was hung over with a mean headache. He'd left the Lotus shortly after Theda stomped out, the night before. Since it had been raining and cold, he decided he deserved a couple more Manhattans. Now, trying to wake up, he fished through his desk drawer looking for the bottle of aspirin in the back behind the box of paper clips and his collection of purloined black and blue ink pens. He flipped off the cap, and swallowed two, choking them down with some old seltzer water in a bottle resting on the filing cabinet. The answering machine began recording the first message of the day.

"Hello Mr. McAllister? This is Theda. I'm sorry I got mad yesterday. Can I make an appointment to see you this morning?" Her voice was girlish, apologetic and pleading.

Frank swung his legs off the couch, placed his feet on the floor, stretching his toes. He looked around for his shoes and ignored the phone. 10:09 A.M. the phone rang again. It was Theda with the same pleading message. 10:10 A.M. the phone rang again. This time Frank answered. He was ready to snarl at her to leave him alone, but instead, he took a deep breath.

"This is McAllister. Whaddaya want now? I don't work without getting paid. I already told you that."

"The G's gave me $500 bucks! They wanna meet you!"

Frank blinked, and reached over to the night stand. He picked up and opened his brown leather wallet with the gold PI badge and stared at the single tattered twenty that remained there.

"Yeah, I'll talk with ya," he said in resignation.

"Oh, thank you Frank, I really appreciate this."

"Meet me at the Lotus in an hour. I'll be getting a bowl of soup. I hope it's the split pea," Frank muttered into the receiver before hanging up. "The kind with lots of little pieces of ham in it" he said to himself.

Frank locked the door to his office and started feeling better. He walked downstairs and flopped down at the end of the bar. Midge was the day bartender. She had worked at the Lotus for as long as anyone could remember. She was pushing sixty, but maintained a good figure and an even better attitude. Her bleached blond hair went past her shoulders, but was far too long for a woman her age. It looked thin and stringy where she hadn't teased it to make it fluffy. She pulled it back loosely securing it with a sterling silver barrette. Midge wore a lot of makeup around the eyes and a pale salmon colored lipstick, applied in a thick layer. Her high end silk white blouse was low cut. The sleeves of the black fuzzy sweater she wore over it were pushed to the elbows.

Midge had large breasts, speckled with age spots and freckles, and didn't mind showing some cleavage. She'd serve drinks and lean over the bar showing the older male customers what they wanted to see.

"These boobs have sold a lot of whiskey," she told Frank once. "And put a few bills in my purse too. If ya don't like it ya don't have to look," she said batting her eyes playfully.

Frank knew Midge was sweet on him but she was a little too worn around the edges for his tastes. The older he got, the less interested he became in chasing set-in-their-ways older women—especially if they had any mileage and the tedious emotional baggage that went with it.

"Looks like you need a "hair of the dog" Frank." Midge said amusedly.

"Yeah. Gimme a tall Bloody Mary and in a few minutes I'll need a bowl of that soup you guys make. Ya got split pea today, with ham, right?"

"Marty said you were in here last night shinin' on some black chick. What's goin' on?"

"Client—it's nothing personal."

"Split pea!" said Midge, nodding, "with ham!"

"And lots of those oyster crackers—three packages and the pepper shaker too, honey."

"Hate to bring it up Frank, but the boss thinks your booze tab is gettin' higher than he's comfortable with. And your office rent is a week late—again!"

Frank sucked long and hard on the Bloody Mary after stirring it with the celery stick, trying to ignore Midge. He drank most of the straight vodka that had settled on the bottom, adding two drops of hot sauce and sucked at the drink a little more. He was concentrating on his drink and nibbling the celery when Theda startled him by flopping down on the stool next to him. She turned, leaning into him and smiled, passing him a white envelope, and sliding it across the countertop silently.

"Five hundred dollars!" she purred in his direction. Frank tapped the envelope looking at Midge, meaningfully.

"I got the money, Boss!" he said.

"I see that," said Midge.

"You know I'm always good for it, right?"

"I hope so," she murmured.

Midge leaned over the bar, deliberately showing more cleavage as she continued polishing the countertop. She looked over at Frank's companion of the moment with a look of disapproval on her face. Theda realized she was being assessed by an older white woman, whose glory days were well behind her. Theda smiled, tilting her head to the side playfully, and exposing straight white teeth. She adjusted her teal V neck sweater, pulling the neck line a little lower and pushing her chest forward. The top of her thin hot-pink bra strap was visible. The pink brassiere strap contrasted nicely with her smooth cocoa skin.

Frank tried to keep a straight face but realized what was happening. The two women were having a tit measuring contest. Frank turned away for a moment until he was sure he could hold back the smile that was threatening to erupt, and asked Theda if she wanted a drink.

"Too early in the day for *me* Mr. McAllister; besides I was up late last night talking to the G's about JoJo's murder." Midge straightened up when she heard the word *murder* but said nothing. She turned and walked away.

"Okay what happens next?" Frank asked.

"Meet me at the Burger Barn on Union Avenue about midnight. The OG's wanna meetcha."

"Tonight?"

"Yeah, Frank, tonight."

Theda scooted off the bar stool without further conversation, strutting out slowly making sure Midge saw her every curve, as she swung her hips girlishly.

"Sexy little bitch!" Midge muttered.

"Thinkin' about tappin' that?" she asked Frank. But Frank was tossing the little crackers into his split pea soup. He shrugged, smiling over at Midge but didn't answer.

"What's an OG Frank?"

"Old gangster," he said, scraping the bottom of the soup bowl.

"Right. I shoulda known that."

"Yep, just an old gangster, Midge. That's all."

The Burger Barn

THE BURGER BARN was a tired, all-night, greasy-spoon burger and coffee shop deep in the Albina ghetto on Union Avenue. The front door opened directly onto the street. Inside was a counter of ten stools, one of which always seemed to be broken. Behind the counter sat a small grill that served up the burgers and a French fryer, and an old one burner coffee pot. A seventy five cent cheese burger was about all they served and they were good. Fries, forty five cents, coffee, thirty cents a cup. Unless you were a cop, then it was free. The night time customers were the black after-hour's crowd and cops looking for a coffee break. They basically ignored each other, each existing in their own little bubble inside the Burger Barn.

The place smelled like it looked: tired, if tired has a smell. With a combination of burger grease and bleach from the sink, it was a good smell nonetheless—a familiar smell to those who knew and liked it. A person could tell by looking that a health inspector rarely entered the Burger Barn. A good idea as all the inspectors tended to be white and shied away from ever going to the ghetto, intentionally. But the Burger Barn was never dirty. It was tiny and well-kept and an appreciated part of the Albina neighborhood.

At the end of the counter sat a dish sink and behind it a wooden door that led to a larger room with a slight but noticeable downward slant from a deteriorating foundation in the back. The floor was covered in sparkling but worn blue and yellow linoleum that accommodated the downward bend of the room by cracking here and there. A flat metal molding was nailed over one long crack, to disguise it.

In the center of the back room was a poker table that seated six. A pile of poker chips lay randomly scattered on the faded green felt, left there by the last winner, or loser. The back room smelled different than the café portion of the Burger Barn. It had the smell of beer and marijuana. A mostly full bottle of whiskey sat on a small refrigerator that when opened revealed two six packs of Old English 800. Next to the whiskey was a stack of old vinyl LP's with Marvin Gaye and Al Green on top. An old Stacy Adams shoe box top which was used for rolling seeds out of the "smoke" lay on the top of the refrigerator as well, collecting dust.

Out the back door, which was secured by a rough-hewn two-by-four that slipped into metal retaining bars for security, were two large garbage dumpsters. At night the dark grey Albina rats could be seen scurrying about looking for hamburger and bread scraps. There were a lot of rats in the ghetto, both rodent and human and it seemed like they were always on the move.

A deeply rutted alley ran behind the Burger Barn. Two abandoned cars, stripped of anything valuable blocked the alley, which was overgrown with brambles, Canadian Thistle, dandelions and a few old rose bushes, leaving a path hardly wide enough to walk through.

The OG's Frank would be meeting were a council of retired gangsters, wild in their youth, and cautious in their old age. They could all look back on youthful recklessness which led to long prison sentences, but now they were retired pensioners, comfortable with their existence and too old to get into trouble.

Roosevelt Jenkins, spent most of *his* youth terrorizing the electric companies in Portland and surrounding areas. This included the telephone companies and all the wire utility companies as well. With his long handled "hot stick" Roosevelt could cut down a thousand feet of phone and utility copper wire in a single night. Wearing his official looking orange utility workers vest, he would roll up the wire and throw it in his truck, a rebuilt and rebuilt-again, *International Harvester* forties something beater. Then he would build a fire in the fireplace at his house to burn the insulation off. To add to the appearance of used copper he would drive over the wire with his truck a few times until he thought it looked nice and dirty, and second hand. He sold the wire to all the scrap metal dealers, some from prominent Jewish families living in Portland and they were *always* willing to buy it, knowing that it was stolen.

Over time, Roosevelt cost the utilities so much insurance money, they hired an investigator to catch him. But he caught himself, so to speak, when on one of his excursions he was burning insulation in the fireplace of his home and it caught his house on fire which burned to the ground. Charged with stealing thousands of dollars of copper wire, Roosevelt was handed down a sentence of five to ten, with time off for good behavior. But his attraction to copper wire and easy money was too much of a temptation. He was undeterred and always went back to his old line of work—copper theft. Eventually, Roosevelt was imprisoned several more times and finally, after so many years of being in the joint, he decided to retire.

Roosevelt was Jojo's grandfather. Roosevelt's *grandson* had been murdered.

The Meeting

RANK PULLED UP in front of the Burger Barn at ten minutes after twelve, midnight. Turning off the ignition he sat for a moment with his hands resting lightly on the steering wheel. With the window rolled down he could smell the night air. Gazing down the street, he remembered the neighborhood and a million recollections came tumbling back. Frank was transported back in time to an altogether different life. Ten years of his life had been spent pushing a squad car through the gloomy streets of the Albina ghetto after dark, and here he was again. Yet, Albina was familiar in a comforting way. It had been home for Frank and he knew its every dimension; every alley and dead-end street, every closed up storefront and old battered house. He even fondly remembered the funny old Monkey tree that sat for decades on North Albina Avenue, only a few blocks from Peninsula Park.

Frank removed the keys from his '69 Dodge Charger, locked it, and looked around checking out the few people lingering on the sidewalks. Deciding his car would be reasonably safe, he entered the Burger Barn. It was empty, so he took a seat at the counter and ordered coffee, placing a dollar bill on the counter.

"It's been a long time since we've seen you in here Officer McAllister," purred a smooth female voice. Frank remembered the old waitress from a few years back.

"I'm waiting for someone. Yes it *has* been a long time. You're looking very well, though."

"Thank you, sir. Would you like coffee in a paper cup for thirty cents or in a regular cup for thirty five cents?

"What's the difference in price? I can't remember."

"Well, I has tuh wash the regular cup," she explained.

"I do seem to recall that was the rule."

"But y'all can have the regular cup for thirty cents, cuz I remember *you*."

Miss Raiford was an older woman in her early sixties with short gray hair, tinted purple. She had an elegant gliding walk that made her dangling black pearl earrings sway back and forth. Frank wondered if she had been a dancer in her younger years, for she was slender and willowy enough to have been a dancer at one time. Miss Raiford was still pretty and wore an attractive shade of pink frost lipstick and frosty blue eye shadow. Frank felt as if he should tip his hat to her, but he wasn't wearing one, so he nodded respectfully instead, as she poured his coffee into the heavy tan coffee cup.

"Thank you, Miss Raiford," Frank murmured quietly. She seemed touched and placed her right hand over her throat, her eyes widening slightly as she gazed at Frank.

"Oh my—you remembered my name? *You* must be the one they sent Theda to fetch."

She smiled knowingly, which told Frank she was in on everything. Frank wasn't sure how he felt about being *fetched* and he contemplated the word for a moment, but only nodded his head in agreement and reached for his coffee cup.

It had been a long time since Frank sat at this counter with a coffee cup cradled in his hands and wearing a cop's uniform. The smells were the same, the bleach and French fry grease, the faint scent of Miss Raiford's Rose perfume and the lingering exhaust that drifted in from the street every time someone opened the door. He wondered at the almost comfortable feeling he had sitting there waiting for something to happen and watching Miss Raiford move elegantly behind the counter, tending to her duties with the graceful fluidity of an old ballet dancer.

A half hour passed, and Miss Raiford topped off Frank's coffee. He was getting nervous, wondering if he had been stood up, or worse yet, set up. He nudged the .45 in its holster on his right hip, beneath his jacket, an old habit from his days as a cop. The ghetto was his element and though he wasn't a cop anymore, he still felt in charge, despite being nervous. He was Frank McAllister and had spent more time in this ghetto and in this restaurant than many of its current residents. Frank was startled by a tugging at his sleeve. Turning sharply, he saw it was Theda.

"Damn woman! You sneak up on me like a ghost. I've been nursing this coffee for almost an hour. Where'd ya come from? I didn't see ya come in."

"I didn't come in. I was in the back room with grandpa. We've been watchin' you."

"Watchin' me?"

"To make sure everything is on the up and up. Us black folks gotta keep an eye out, ya know?" Frank stood up and glanced out front to make sure his Charger was still intact.

"Maybe I should just go," he said, standing up and taking a step toward the door.

"Wait, what do ya mean?"

"I'm not sure about all this."

"Don't worry about your car. We got some brothers watchin' it. They know you're here to help," Theda said softly.

"Don't leave Mr. McAlister—just hear us out."

Frank turned to the voice and saw that is was Miss Raiford. She stood near the coffee pot watching. Frank looked at her pleading half-smile and hopeful eyes and knew he wouldn't leave. A little more relaxed now, Frank allowed Theda to usher him into the back room showing him where to sit at the poker table. He sat in a chair across from three older men; a chair that was well worn but comfortable. The kind of comfortable that comes from much use and it was just the correct height for dealing cards.

"Welcome Mr. McAllister. I'm Roosevelt. This is Mr. Candy, Theda's Grandfather, and Neon, Mr. Neon Jones."

Frank acknowledged each man in turn with a gracious nod of his head as he shook each man's hand. He looked closely at their faces trying to read their eyes. They seemed friendly but serious.

"I've seen you all before," Frank said with a slow smile. He waited for their reaction and grinned as a quiet twitter of chuckles arose from the three men.

"I used to have a collection of mug shots. I kept it in the back of my patrol car."

"I bet you did. I bet you did," said Mr. Candy, laughing quietly.

"I've seen you all around, though that *was* a long time ago."

"Here, have a drink Officer McAllister."

"Just call me Frank."

Mr. Candy pushed a bottle of Jack Daniels across the table, followed by a shot glass. The offer to drink sounded like the command that it was. Frank knew the routine and poured a shot and casually tossed it back as the G's watched. A can of Old English slid across the table.

"Here's a little chaser if ya need it," said Mr. Candy, encouragingly.

"I could always use a chaser," Frank said with a smile.

Frank shook off the first shot and then tossed down another. After a few swallows of ice cold Old English, Frank sat the can on the table in front of him and looked across at his hosts.

"Ya didn't invite me here just to drink so what's the deal? What's up?" The three old men looked at each other as if deciding who the spokesman should be, and then Roosevelt began.

"Sorry about the way we gotcha here, but we needs help. Folks here in Albina bein' robbed and murdered and the cops ain't doing nothin' bout it. We sent Theda here, to round you up cause we figgered a pretty girl might have a better chance at convincin' ya to help us, than jus a few old guys. If one of us showed our ugly old face in your office…well, ya know?"

"Ah, I'm not like that," Frank said with a chuckle. He took the time to look each man in the eye. He was feeling the shots and realized he'd been sucked in, "fetched" according to Miss Raiford by Theda, a pretty young black woman, but there were worse things that could happen.

"So, why *me?*" he asked blandly.

"We knows you was a cop and we 'preciate you kep' things pretty straight when you was workin' here back in the old days. We knows you kicked ass when ass needed to be kicked and the ghetto folks were down with dat. But now our community here is bein' terrorized by this here murderin' gangsta, but we don't know who he is!" said Candy.

"The prick murdered my Grandson, Jojo!" Roosevelt interjected, angrily.

"That's right—Jojo!" Theda echoed quietly.

"And he tried to catch my granddaughter Theda, here," said Candy.

"Whoever this guy is, he's crossin' the line!" Neon said, speaking up for the first time.

"That's right, he crossin' the line!" Roosevelt hissed angrily.

"He murdered four black folk, all out late, all drunk tryin' tuh get home from the after-hour club. Just regular folks, just trying to have fun, and now Jojo! Five folks murdered!" Neon muttered.

"And the cops don't care. They ain't doin' shit about it. Sayin' it's jus grudges done by other black folks, and so it don't matter, none!"

"You have to find the guy!" said Theda. Frank pushed back in his chair and took a deep breath.

"You're all looking for...I dunno, for some kind of Paladin," said Frank.

"Who's Paladin?" they all asked, almost in unison.

"You remember the old TV show, Paladin? Have gun will travel? The good town folks would hire Paladin to come in and do battle with the evil sheriff who was in cahoots with the cattle rustlers, or some such? He cleaned up the town usually after a gun battle or two." Frank poured himself another shot and settled back into the chair scooting it closer to the table.

"But Paladin worked for free. I don't. I have rent to pay. Besides my regular work will suffer if I take your case. So, what's the pay, if I may be so crass as to ask about money?"

"What is yer regular work McAllister?" Candy asked smoothly.

"I do a lot of skip tracing, ya know, trackin' down guys that run off with another woman. Husband's ditchin' naggin' wives, that sorta thing. Most of this kinda work is done in the court house and on the phone during the day. Then at night I repo expensive cars for banks—Caddies, Mercedes, Porsches, mostly from guys in the west hills and Lake Oswego. Ya know, the high rent district?"

"How's the work lately?" Theda asked meaningfully.

"Not great, but it's regular. These executive wanna-be's finance a high-end car they can't afford. You know, to keep up appearances. And when they can't make payments any-more they can't let go of that fancy ride. So I prowl around at night, find 'em, tow 'em, and make the bank happy. I get almost a grand each. Been findin' about one a month, two if I'm lucky."

"*If* you're lucky, Frank," said Theda.

"Well, it pays the bills, and my bar tab, too. That's me, so what's *your* story? You're all ex-cons. I can tell by lookin' and as I said I remember your mug shots. I put a few folks in the joint when I worked the North End. I was hard on the heroin dealers too as I recollect, and I won't help you if you're dealin' smack. You need to know that up front. Likewise, if Jojo was killed in a dope murder or a dope deal gone bad? I *won't* help!"

"We are what ya see McAllister. And we *do* recall you didn't like them smack dealers, none. But that was somethin' we never did for business. We were all small time compared to *those* cats."

"Arson was my specialty. And in the off times I made a lot of money filing bogus income tax returns. Went to federal prison a few times for that, but never got caught for burnin' down bidnesses for the insurance money. Those were the good old days," said Neon Jones thoughtfully.

Theda surreptitiously lit a joint and blew the smoke away from the table. She had heard all the stories about her grandfather Mr. Candy and the other OG's numerous times before. She knew how Neon Jones got his nickname—from an old girlfriend who used to travel with him. Sugarcane called him *Neon* because of the excited glimmer in his eyes when a large business went up in flames and he knew he had a successful insurance claim in the works.

Neon always made sure the insurance covered the employee's pay until the business was rebuilt. No one got hurt that way, except the insurance company and they were owned by white folks so that didn't matter. And Mr. Candy was a Cadillac thief. Candy stole new Cadillac's from rental agencies or car dealers with stolen credit cards. Theda's grandfather would drive the stolen Caddies to Atlanta or Miami where he'd sell them to folks who didn't care about the particulars of legitimate ownership. Most of the cars went directly to Cuba. Then upon leaving, Candy would steal another Caddie in Miami and drive it back to Portland. "Never did git stopped. People don't think nothin' bout seeing a niggah in a Cadillac smokin' a cee-gar," Candy told Theda once.

"What are ya worried about Officer McAllister? You seem a might nervous," said Neon.

"I'm fine, don't worry about *me*."

"Are ya sure about that, McAllister?"

"I'm just fine Neon. So, what are you driving these days? I seem to remember you had a fondness for long bright orange Cadillac's."

"Maybe that nice Dodge Charger parked out front my boys have been lookin' at!" Candy said, slapping his thigh and laughing. All the OG's joined in the merriment enjoying Frank's discomfort. Frank was not as amused as he let on and was in a hurry to get down to business.

"So, what's the story on this guy that's robbin' and killin' the neighborhood folks?"

"We been callin' him...well, we been callin' him *Batman*. I know it's kinda silly, but its cause he sneaks up on the folks he robs," said Roosevelt.

"He pulls up in his car; no lights on, wearing only black clothes, motor off, and coasts to a stop. Then he opens up the passenger door and demands they money or drugs, or both. He barely says nothin'. Lets his .38 do the talkin' for him. Folks he robs are always drunk coming out of the after-hours places. Usually too messed up and embarrassed to complain to the po-lice if they don' get shot. And the po-lice don't do nothin' noways, anyhow."

"He shot my grandson Jojo!" Roosevelt burst out.

"Jojo musta told him to fuck off and started runnin'. Blam! Blam! Blam! He shot Jojo three times in the back. Died on the corner of Commercial and Skidmore. Just like that, with his hand in the gutter. Died with his hand in a puddle of cold rain water. Just like that—just like that. My boy! My grandson!"

"And he tried to catch me too!" said Theda quietly, looking over at Frank with wide eyes.

"You too?"

"Yeah! He snuck up on me with his lights off as I was comin' out of Van's Olympic Room. As soon as I saw the gun come out, I run fast, dippin' and dodgin' up the alley and beat it between some houses. He just came outa' nowhere." Frank took the last swig of the whiskey bottle and set if back on the table.

"Batman huh?" Frank asked, bemusedly. "That's a funny name you gave him. Guess it fits."

"Yeah," said Neon, "and like a insult the dude throws the empty wallet in the street and drives over it, slinkin' away with his lights off, turns at the corner and disappears into the night. Sometimes leavin' a dead body there, too!"

"Any idea who this jerk is, any word on the street?" asked Frank.

"Folks think he might be some out-of-towner," said Roosevelt. "Maybe a gangsta from Seattle, or maybe Vegas. We just doesn't know. No one gets a good look at the dude cause he wears a ski-mask and pulls the hood of his coat over his face. Let's his gun do all the talkin'. Can't tell if Batman is black nor white neither, cause he's always all covered up."

"Murdered my Jojo. We need to git dis bastard! We need to git em' and nail him to the wall!" Roosevelt slammed his fist down hard on the table and the empty whiskey bottle fell over.

"Let ma boy die on the street corner—wit his hand in the gutter! My boy! My boy! Bitch mutherfucker!" Roosevelt's lower lip began to tremble and he looked down embarrassed, clasping his hands tightly in his lap, his shoulders hunched.

By the time the meeting was over, the bottle of Jack was gone and the Old English was gone. It was beginning to break daylight and Frank was a little drunk and more than a little tired. He stood up, shook all their hands and said he'd be in touch. He walked out the door, turning and nodding politely to Miss Raiford as she sat on a stool, reading a fashion magazine. She smiled sweetly and waved back at him with two long elegant fingers, "You take care Officer McAllister" she murmured.

Standing on the sidewalk Frank smelled the freshness of a new dawn. The scent of green moss, flowers and car exhaust seemed to blend together to form the unique smell of the Albina he remembered. He turned and stood looking North on Union and sniffed the fragrant air, but more carefully now. He remembered the faint but distinct smell of burning flesh—what they used to call the "Albina Barbecue," a stink so familiar to him at one time. Frank knew Lips McGriffin was still running his crematorium. He smiled and reminded himself to get in touch with Lips and see if he had any kind of lead on this Batman character. Squinting against the morning sun and the inevitability of another long day Frank contemplated just exactly what he had agreed to get mixed up in.

Paladin-Paladin, where do you roam?
Paladin-Paladin, where is your home?

Paladin Takes the Case

I T WAS EXACTLY 2:13 P.M., the following day when the phone rang in Frank's office at the Lotus. He had a headache from drinking with the OG's. The answering machine picked up and it was Theda.

"Frank! Are you awake yet? It's after two and I've got money for you. I'm downstairs."

Frank searched his pockets for his Marlboro's, found one in the package and then looked around for his Zippo. He spotted it on the floor near his brown, size eleven wingtips where it had fallen during the night. He reached down, picked it up and flipped it open, but the lid fell off as the hinge was broken again. Searching in the back of his desk drawer, Frank found a thin paper clip and twisted off a small piece, making a new hinge for the Zippo and positioning it carefully into place. He flipped the lighter a couple of times to make sure it worked and then lit his cigarette. He sat on the couch, and coughed while struggling to slip on his shoes. The pale blue smoke drifted up toward the sunlight streaming in from the large windows and back lighting the many dust motes that danced in the sunlit air.

Locking the door behind him, Frank picked his way down the stairs, gripping the railing, a little more unsteady than he wanted to admit, and slowly entered the barroom. He saw Theda standing off to the side of the bar waiting for him and dressed to the nines in a low cut light blue polka dot dress with black satin flats. He walked to the bar and sat down, running his hands through his wavy hair and rubbing the scruff on his face. Theda looked gorgeous as she slid onto the stool next to him.

"Here's your money!" she said hopefully, smiling and pushing another envelope at him. Frank pushed it back.

"I haven't made up my mind yet, I'm not sure I wanna be your Paladin."

"Oh come on Frank! We need yer help, man. No one else can do it." She was pleading, her large eyes bright, luminous and intensely feminine.

"I'm not sure about workin' for three old convicts. I just don't know yet. I'm gonna have to think on it."

"Frank, they're not gangsters any more. Not now anyways. They're just old businessmen. They each run their own after-hours club. They sell booze at night. They have poker games. They sell a little weed. It's the *white man* who wants people to stop drinkin' at two thirty. It's the *white man* who don't allow gambling lessn' he gits a piece of it."

"Theda honey, keep your voice down in here. No sense talkin' politics."

"You know it's true, Frank. It's the *white man* who says pot is bad. Shit, us black folks know better-n-that. The G's never stuck a gun in nobody's face and took money—not like that murderin' Batman. The G's ripped off the insurance companies, and the government. Their business was rippin' the white man and makin' a livin'. So fuckin' what!" Theda was more agitated by her outburst than she realized. She took a deep breath.

"Are you guys gonna order a drink or what?" Midge asked, standing back but listening intently.

"I'll have a Bloody Mary," Frank replied.

"Coffee for me," said Theda, politely.

"Comin' up!"

"Frank was out late last night, I think he's gotta headache. Ya got any aspirin back there, Midge?"

Midge rolled her eyes but reached around and slapped a Bayer aspirin bottle in front of Frank. He opened the bottle, tossed three into his palm and swallowed them with his drink.

He had brought a cigarette in with him and was now looking for an ashtray to put it out. Midge reached below the counter and slid one in front of him. It was clear, she was anxious to hear more of their conversation, while pretending she didn't care. She went back to polishing glasses and looking over old credit card receipts.

Frank decided the topic of conversation wasn't something he wanted Midge to hear and Theda pushing an envelope at him full of money was *not* what he wanted Midge to see either. He nudged Theda, glancing at her meaningfully. She understood and they finished their drinks in silence, got up after a moment and left. Midge realized she'd been caught eavesdropping and retreated to the far end of the bar where she washed shot glasses and swiped her bar towel at imaginary dust motes in the air. She was pretending not to care but it bothered her to see Frank with a much younger and beautiful woman.

"Aiya hiyoo!" A yelp coming from Indian Charlie sitting in the back booth intruded on the moment.

"Who is the split tail with Frank?" Charlie asked Midge as the pair left.

"Oh, you shut up Charlie! And get outa here! Besides you're rude. Split tail?!"

"Come on Midge, sell old Indian Charlie a whiskey."

"Charlie you know I can't sell you anything but coffee. *You're* interdicted!"

"Fuck the white man! Tellin' me if I can drink or not? Where's your interdiction list so I can wipe my ass with it?"

Midge continued polishing the bar for something to do as she watched Charlie, an old Warm Springs Indian wobble out the door. Charlie Horse or *Charlie-Rides-The-Horse*, as he gave his true name was frail. He was an older man in his sixties and wore his black hair in one long braid that fell to his waist. The braid was slightly frayed from having been slept on too many times without being combed.

When Charlie had a little money at the first of the month he'd buy a round trip ticket and take the Greyhound from the Warm Springs Indian reservation ninety five miles away to Portland. There, he would rent a room at the Lotus down the hall from Frank near the bathroom and hang out in the tenderloin until he ran out of money. Since Charlie-Rides-The-Horse was on the Oregon Liquor Control Commission's list of interdicted persons, he was not allowed to drink alcohol in Oregon. In protest, Charlie would hang out at the Blind Pig, an unlicensed drinking establishment and the best kept secret of a still caring tenderloin neighborhood.

FRANK AND THEDA silently trudged up the stairs and walked down the hall. The carpet was so thick they didn't make as much as a sound as they walked, opening the door to room number ten. The smell of stale air and old cigarette smoke filled Theda's nose, as she entered the room. Frank didn't seem to notice the stale smell as he walked behind the desk and flopped down on the couch. He leaned back, stretched and then leaned forward resting his elbows on his knees. He seemed slightly embarrassed at the tawdry condition of the room, looking around at the dust bunnies drifting on the unswept floor and the general clutter.

Theda stood in the center of the room, then walked to the sofa and seated herself next to Frank. She turned and casually began brushing tiny flakes of dandruff off Frank's shoulders. It was an impulsive act of easy familiarity, but it surprised Frank and he pulled away slightly, looking over and smiling shyly. The moment was awkward but they said nothing. Theda turned to the beaded purse in her lap and removed a fat envelope and thrust it at Frank with a quick, disingenuous smile. She was stressed and Frank knew it.

"You *know* you're the only one can help and maybe find out who killed Jojo." Frank took a deep breath and looked down at his calloused hands, trying to formulate the words he needed to say.

"Theda! Honey!"

"Yes?"

"I spent ten years workin' that garbage dump of a neighborhood, paid for with the citizen's money. Workin' for the OG's goes against my sense of—oh, I dunno..." His voice trailed off.

"Against what, Frank? You know the regular police won't help us. They don't care, Frank. You *know* that. You know they don't care about black folk. Even the one or two black guys on the force don't care about *us!* They think *all* black folks in Albina are crooked."

"Theda, I got nothin' but bad memories of Albina. Women I used to know, a couple I shoulda married but didn't. Dirty cops, harmless three time losers bein' killed that *shouldn't* have been—the vice guys getting' away with it? Gettin' away with murder? My past, Theda, it's all tied up there, every street, practically every damn avenue or alley way. I know every inch like the back of my hand but there's no good feeling left. Can you understand that?"

Frank leaned back on the sofa and stared straight ahead at the wall, across the room, adorned only with an out of date, yellowing Farmers insurance company calendar which hung askew and was several years out of date.

"But it's not *like* that anymore Frank. You're not a cop anymore. You were...you were freed from that whole scene. You're off the hook in certain ways. The G's only want justice for the community, and for our families. You'd be workin' for us—for the little people. That Batman is a murderer. The cops ain't doin' nothin about it. And you know they won't, cause they don't give a damn!"

Theda was pleading again, absently touching the shoulder of his second hand blazer as she sat next to him. Frank took the envelope from her, fingering it, turning it over in his hands. He felt the crinkly paper and opened it enough to see it contained a lot of green. He slipped it in the breast pocket of his jacket reluctantly.

"Okay," he said quietly, sighing in resignation. Theda looked up sharply at the ceiling and exhaled heavily. The relief she emanated was palpable, intense and heartbreaking.

"Thank you Frank. Thank you so much!"

"I gotta figure out a plan, though. And it ain't gonna be easy. I'm gonna need to keep a low profile. The cops can't know anything about it, or that I'm in any way involved. You understand that?"

"Yes! Of course!"

"And you're all gonna have to wait for me to get things straight in my head, and not pressure me about it, okay?"

"Absolutely. No problem. Whatever you want."

Frank was slightly irritated he had been sucked into a potentially dangerous agreement by Theda, a female Trojan horse with a fat envelope full of money. But now that he was in it he'd have to figure out how to track down a killer and not end up on the department's radar at the same time.

"You tell the old men I'll help. I'll do my best but I can't make any promises to you or anyone, understood?"

"Yes! Good! I'll tell my grandfather Candy that you're gonna help!" Theda said brightly. She was gazing straight into Frank's eyes, elated and euphoric, a hopeful smile on her face.

"Has anyone told you—you really have what they call "smoky" blue eyes?" It was the eye contact that sealed the deal. Frank knew there would be no going back.

"Well? Has anyone ever told you that, Frank?"

"Ah, come on honey. Don't do that."

"Don't do *what* Frank?"

"You know perfectly well what, Theda."

Charlie-Rides-The-Horse
and the Blind Pig

FUCKIN' INTERDICTION SHIT!" Charlie muttered bitterly, gazing blankly at the stained wall of his room. It was morning and Charlie desperately needed a drink to get his day started properly. He knew better than to coax a drink out of Midge at the bar. So, leaving his room door open he walked to the adjacent bathroom and locked the door behind him. He ran cold water over his head and face, dried off his dripping black hair with some paper towels and stared at his reflection in the cracked mirror.

In the ancient crumbling mirror he saw an older Indian man with light brown skin, still smooth for his age except for the wrinkles around his eyes and forehead. On his chin sprouted six or seven hairs. The black hair, near his temples had just enough grey strands to be noticeable. Cupping his hand under the cold water he rinsed his mouth and rubbed his index finger back and forth over his teeth in an effort to clean them. Charlie knew he reeked of alcohol but he would be drinking soon so he figured it wouldn't matter anyway. He had a headache from drinking too many Mickey's of *Gallo Tokay* wine he'd scored the night before from a bum whose name he couldn't remember. He knew the headache would go away after a couple of good whiskeys.

Hanging around his neck on a deer hide string was a black obsidian arrow head, which Charlie had made as a youth. It was shiny, sharp and translucent when held up to the light. He reached up and gripped the arrow head between the fingers of his right hand. By pushing it into his thumb and forefinger, he could feel the sting and might even see a spot of blood, and would know if it was still of value.

He decided to test the point with his thumb, and proceeded to push down, almost piercing the skin. As he felt the pain he knew if it was attached to a strong Pine shaft it could still pierce the eye of a Magpie.

Satisfied the arrow head was still of value, Charlie decided he would give it to his friend, Old George. He had money to spend with George and was looking forward to it. He turned and walked out of the bathroom, headed back to his room and closed the door behind him, not bothering to lock it. The only thing of value in his room was his return ticket to Warm Springs and it was hidden under the corner of the frayed rug beneath the bed.

Standing on the sidewalk in front of the Lotus, Charlie retrieved a pouch of Sir Walter Raleigh crimp-cut tobacco and a pack of Top rolling papers and slowly fashioned a smokable cigarette. A discarded book of matches he found in the bathroom lit the first smoke of the day. It was near 11: A.M. and the sun was burning off some foggy Portland clouds when Charlie noticed two metal doors of a sidewalk elevator slowly open. He was looking directly across Third Avenue at a familiar sight.

As the elevator reached the sidewalk and stopped, Charlie smiled broadly and waved to his friend George sitting in his wheel chair across the road. George, at street level from the basement shielded his eyes from the harsh daylight. As the owner of The Blind Pig, which was an unlicensed drinking establishment, George had to keep its existence quiet. The Oregon Liquor Control or the "liquor dicks" as they were called had been searching for his little hole in the wall for some time. Some of the nondrinking neighborhood residents heard rumors about The Blind Pig, but could never discover its location, right out in plain sight.

Charlie knew, as did the entire neighborhood, the sad story of three years before. George and his wife Alice had been struck by a hit and run driver. They stood at the crosswalk a block from the Lotus at nearby SW third and Taylor, having just come from their room at the Hamilton Hotel. Way Lum, a local business owner witnessed the accident and the bloody mess afterward. Lum had tried to help, but Alice died at the scene. George was sent to Oregon Health Sciences University hospital but a spinal injury left him confined permanently to a wheel chair. Lum was devastated by what he'd seen at the very door of his small café. He swept up glass and a small chunk of chrome and hosed away the blood, while fighting back tears thinking of George and his sweet-tempered wife Alice, who always had a smile on her face. Determined to do what he could for the newly crippled widower, George, Mr. Lum decided to let him live in basement of the café and make it comfortable and homey, with lower rent than normal. The basement floor of the old Chinese café was smooth concrete and was easy for George to negotiate in his new wheel chair. Lum also agreed it would be a good idea if George sold a little beer and whiskey, in secret of course and for a few of the ordinary people, a small number of the locals who lived in the tenderloin, and frequented Mr. Lum's café.

The liquor dicks never did pick up any rumors about The Blind Pig. It was a secret deal and only a handful of people knew. George used the freight elevator to get up to street level every morning and do his daily shopping, with the bags stuffed discreetly in the back of his wheel chair. The few customers used the alley door hidden behind a stack of pallets by the big dumpster to go down, and knock on the basement door. It started out as a casual meeting place for friends of George and some quiet neighbors and in time, The Blind Pig was born.

The After-Hours Joint

ROOSEVELT PRIDED HIMSELF on owning and operating the fanciest after-hours in Albina and the most consistently undetected by vice cops. The house was on North Kerby Street two houses in from North Blandena. From the front it looked like it should be demolished. The old wooden porch was sagging and leaning away from the foundation. All the windows except the front window were broken. The cracked windows were taped over with silver duct tape. Whatever colors the house had been long ago weathered away and disappeared, becoming an indistinct grey. The concrete steps were cracked and large chunks were missing. An abandoned and parted out junker decorated the street in front. It was a rusted sixties Chevy with the VIN number cut out. What little patches of grass remained were losing the competition with the weeds, brambles and Canadian Thistle. For Roosevelt's purposes his house was perfect in appearance and location.

As 2:00 A.M. approached, Roosevelt was getting everything set up for the night's business. The glass backed bar was stocked with American bourbon whiskey, Canadian blends, Vodka, both expensive Russian and cheap Oregon Monarch. There was English Gin and of course Hennessey's. Ice cold Coors and Budweiser along with Steele Reserve and Old English 800 sat in a well-stocked refrigerator in the kitchen. Roosevelt included a bottle of wine or two but his clientèle usually didn't drink wine, preferring the hard stuff, instead. Marijuana joints were also for sale, at two dollars a doobie. Two six person poker tables were set up in the front room, prepared with new decks of poker cards and stacks of chips neatly contained in brown plastic chip caddies.

All the windows were covered in blackout shades sealed with tape. The ugly but necessary black shades were covered by elegant royal blue sateen draperies with fancy wood sliders at the top. The floor was covered with plush burgundy carpet, so thick it left tracks when walked on. A Neon Bubble jukebox sat out of the way in a corner emanating a faint pink aura. Five plays for a dollar—BB King, Al Green, Marvin Gaye and Miles Davis could all be heard.

Seating was available with comfortable, expensive looking couches including a beige camel-back model from the early sixties, with a slim elegant spine. Two person love seats dotted most of the other available spaces in the large room, all plush and so comfortable you didn't want to get up once you sank into them. It was late and Roosevelt was ready for business.

Outside cars were starting to collect, parking all over the neighborhood and in front of the houses along the street. Access to this after-hours club was from the dirt alley that ran behind Kerby Street and into the back of the house via a set of old wooden stairs.

People walked up the alley, talking quietly and smoking, waiting in line behind the already gathering patrons. A flask or two could be seen glittering in the dim glow of cigarettes. Theda was guiding Frank by the arm as they walked up the alley, behind Kerby Street, with the gravel crunching dryly under their feet. After knocking, the doorman, a face Frank briefly remembered from meeting the OG's at the Burger Barn stared back at him. Admittance was with the okay of Roosevelt. The black nightlife was waking up. The legit bars were closed and it was now time to party. They came in through the back door. The doorman looked at Frank and Frank looked at the sign, *No Guns Allowed* on the wall to his right.

"He's with me, its okay," Theda said, as she gently pushed Frank ahead of her and into the room.

Frank nudged his Colt .45 1911 with his elbow to make sure it was still there and walked into Roosevelt's night club as if he were walking into an alternate universe of colorful luxury, and comfort. Frank was impressed. The expensive draperies, the plush carpets, and the gold and green sateen wall paper seemed rich and stylish, indeed. For a second Frank thought he was in the posh Benson Hotel where he sometimes went for dinner when he wasn't broke.

He liked the selection behind the bar too, and the juke box added just the right touch. Roosevelt pushed some buttons and "Peaches and Herb" started playing. Frank noticed some incense burning in a china dish on a corner table. The intoxicating scent of Patchouli filled the room. Theda guided Frank to a small love seat in a dim corner where they could see all the action but remain unnoticed. She shoved a shot glass of Hennessey's at him.

"You gonna need a chaser, Frank?"

"Nah, I'm alright."

Frank downed the shot in one gulp, and when it hit bottom he wished he'd agreed on that chaser, but now it would make him look green, so he said nothing, just smiling easily instead. Frank noticed the stares. It was impossible not to stare at him. He was the only white person in the room. Theda looked sternly at the people staring and bristled.

"He works for us. He's okay!" she mouthed, glowering, eyes wide.

Theda was getting pissed off at the blatant curiosity and as soon as she mouthed the words, they turned away and stopped being nosy. Theda crowded against Frank in the love seat, as if to make her point, slipping her arm thorough his and laying it across his lap, proprietarily. Frank was beginning to enjoy her company and the surroundings. Theda smelled good and she felt good sitting next to him, crowded up close, the heat from her thigh warming him. She validated his being there and he couldn't help but notice how long, and silky her slender legs looked as she sat dressed in a pair of tight red Capri's and a light blue pullover.

After an hour and a few more shots the crowd relaxed, people began to play poker, and began smoking pot. The room was filled with the smell of alcohol, incense and tobacco and marijuana smoke. The smoke curled towards the ceiling, in bluish tendrils. As the clients chugged the Old English Frank realized in a quick moment of clarity that Roosevelt was merely a business man. He was providing entertainment and relaxation for his black clientèle on *their* terms and on *their* hours and income for himself and his family. If Batman was murdering these folks and if he killed Jojo, Frank would *be* their Paladin.

The evening ended with Frank and Theda driving to her tidy girlish looking studio apartment. The Paramount apartment was a three-story, 1920s brick building two blocks east of the Willamette River on North Broadway. Her third floor apartment was old style, with a pull-down Murphy bed and a claw foot bath tub. More intoxicated than they realized, Theda fell asleep lying across the double bed and Frank crashed on the couch, his long legs sprawled across the cushions and onto the floor, his arms folded neatly across his chest.

Orange Marmalade in the Morning

F RANK AWOKE TO the smell of coffee drifting through the small apartment. The back window was open and the muslin curtain drifted with the intermittent passing of a light breeze. He checked to make sure he was fully dressed and put his feet on the glossy, clean hardwood floor. He could hear Theda in the bathroom, running water in the sink. She was humming the Peaches and Herb tune, *Reunited*. Frank remembered it from the night before on the jukebox. He needed to pee and felt awkward, wanting to use the toilet. Theda came out of the bathroom.

"Your turn!" she said, in a sing-song voice.

"Thank you, Miss."

"Just put the toilet seat back down when you're through, okay hon?"

"Will do."

Frank peed and washed his hands and face with a fresh bar of Ivory soap, splashing the cool water from the faucet onto his face and neck. He cupped some cold water into his mouth and gargled and spat into the sink. Walking silently into the kitchen, he patted his face and neck with a pink towel and sat at the small table. Draping the towel around his neck, he sat down to drink the coffee Theda pushed across the table.

"Want some toast?"

"Sure. You got any strawberry jam?"

"No, just Orange marmalade."

"I hate marmalade, but I'll take the toast, anyway."

"You should try it, Frank. It's different but after a while you develop a *taste* for it." Theda smiled brazenly at Frank.

He laughed and the look on his face said, *are you crazy?* But Frank felt good being with Theda, and happy to be eating breakfast and drinking coffee with such a pleasant looking girl so early in the morning.

"We gotta have a plan!" Frank said, sitting up straight, looking serious and slapping his hands together as he swallowed a mouthful of buttered toast. His brow was knit together, giving his face another character line, and his jaw a new angle of determination.

"Okay. What are ya thinking?"

"If I'm gonna catch this *Batshit* bastard we just need a plan." Frank sipped his coffee.

"They call him *Batman*, Frank, not batshit."

"Oh, right, sorry. Yes, it *is* Batman."

"Whatcha doin?" Theda asked, after a moment's silence.

"Just thinkin' The only way to catch this guy is to catch him in the act! Catch him dead bang, so to speak." Frank grinned as he was figuring it out in his mind.

"We'll have to get him to rob me. Then I'll have him cold. A sting operation, like how we did it when I was a cop."

"So, how do we do it?"

"Simple. I'll dress shabby, act drunk and hang out around the after-hours clubs or even the legit bars after they close. Then when he hits on me, I got him."

"Sounds dangerous Frank, I dunno, this worries me." Frank gave her a sidelong '*don't forget who you're talking to*' look and Theda smiled knowingly.

"I'm a big boy. Don't worry, I can handle myself. I got ma mits, my 1911 and my tin PI badge. But first I gotta go downtown to the detective office and see if I can find out somethin' about these murders. Then we can implement my plan. First things first, though."

Up the Sidewalk and Into Daylight

CHARLIE HORSE HAD a distinct lean to the right as he walked. His right leg and hip were injured from a fall from a horse when he was a kid on the reservation. When Charlie was drunk he appeared to be in constant danger of falling over as he shuffled along the street and it was obvious he was in constant pain.

He wore gray sweat pants, tied in front with a length of thin cotton rope. The pants were soiled from many days wearing and were too long causing the legs to hang in tatters over his tennis shoes. A faded blue jean-jacket hung open in front showing a white tee-shirt with an Eagle on the front and a depiction of four Indians with rifles under which read *Custer Had It Coming!*

Charlie hurried toward the corner, waving and smiling as George wheeled across Third Avenue. George waited while Charlie pushed him up and over the threshold into Dinty Moore's, maneuvering the wheel chair carefully. Dinty's opened in the mornings for breakfast, serving eggs, bacon and strong Boyd's coffee to the residents of the tenderloin, and particularly those who were hung over and hungry from the night's drinking.

The two men greeted each other with Charlie bending over to give George a half-hug and George shaking Charlie's hand. "How?" said George mimicking a TV Indian as he held up his right hand grinning at Charlie. "I know how! I jus wanna know when, white man!" The two laughed, grinning broadly and continued shaking hands. It was clear to anyone these were two men who liked each other and were comfortable in the other's presence. Charlie pushed the wheel chair close to the table for George, and waited for the waitress to walk over. With a smile on his face, Charlie ordered coffee, eggs, toast and bacon for two.

Snooping at Headquarters

THE OLD WOOD and glass doors of the Police Headquarters building at 209 SW Oak had the familiarity of a good friend or the bad feel of a recurring nightmare, depending. As Frank pulled on the brass handle, he remembered the door was heavy and opened with the same tired squeak. *Police Headquarters,* painted in gold letters on the glass remained unchanged and Frank wondered how many decades it had been there. He figured he'd ask around up in the dicks and see if he could get any information about the killings and particularly about Jojo—if he could find someone who would be willing to talk that is.

It had been twelve years since Frank walked out these same doors with his last pay check, an ex-cop and a free man. He remembered, all at once, the sense of anger and elation as the doors closed behind him for the last time.

It seemed like a long time ago—it seemed like yesterday.

The remaining anger still felt like acid in his belly sometimes, but it had diminished somewhat with the passage of time. The lobby was busy with uniformed cops in search of their patrol cars and others ushering in handcuffed prisoners headed for the jail on the fifth floor. A few nodded at Frank without speaking, old guys he'd worked with who still remembered him. He was a familiar face to some, but a stranger among the new rank and file.

Frank jogged up the marble stairs to the second floor and walked the long hallway back to the detective office on the Pine street side of the building. The building smelled the same, like tired paper and polished Oak. The marble floor was worn from years of being walked on and cleaned with soap and bleach by the night-time janitors. Frank remembered they were all city workers wearing green uniforms while they swept and mopped. They barely looked up from their menial tasks as officers walked by. Sometimes their faces showed the embarrassment of the difference in class. Mostly, the janitors were old black men and Frank always felt sad for them as they pushed their brooms around waiting to get off work, and go home.

Frank wondered how many miles he had walked on this same floor, or how many times he had walked this hall. He wondered how many times he had strolled through the main entrance, but couldn't even guess at a possible number.

The homicide office was open. The gold lettering on the open door left no doubt who was in charge. It read, *Lt. Hatch Homicide Detail Commander.* Three or four detectives including Cunningham were shuffling papers, and filing cases while talking on the phone. Frank walked in uninvited and sat down at a vacant desk. Cunningham was so startled to see Frank he stood up nervously pushing his chair back so suddenly it crashed to the floor, getting the attention of the other detectives in the office.

"McAllister! What are *you* doin' here? You don't belong in here. Get the hell out!"

"Relax Cunningham," Frank replied, nonplussed. "I'm here to see a detective about a missing person. I'm workin' a skip trace."

"I told you..."

"Hey, Frank, good to see ya again, man!"

It was Lieutenant Hatch from the old days when Frank was a patrolman at North. Hatch turned to look at Cunningham sharply with a look that said *I'm in charge here so shut up!*

"Hiya, old man!" Frank replied, "Rumors of your death were wrong I see. Still drivin' that cherry 69 Cad?"

"Yeah, and it still runs good, too. You remember the Humpty Dumpty brothers who worked graveyard at North—Kenny and Lenny? Well they own an auto parts store and garage out on Union and they keep my car up for me. It's the least they can do since I covered for 'em in a few scrapes they got messed up in workin' the street. They were more stupid than crooked ya know?"

"Yeah, I remember the stupid part with those two."

"But I got two more years to go to retire and that's all I care about. How ya doin' Frank? I miss seein' ya around."

"I'm doin' okay Lieutenant, I'm workin'." Lieutenant Hatch offered Frank a sip from a whiskey flask he was holding in his lap. Frank waved it aside.

"Nah, I'm on a case right now."

"Me too said Hatch," with a smirk, looking at his watch and taking a long pull from the flask. "At least for a few more minutes. We should have a drink when I get off."

"Sounds good, but can you help me with some information? What do you know about a black kid shot in the back and killed over on Commercial a while back? I don't think he's been identified. The Oregonian didn't write about it."

"Yeah, there have been a few, but the paper puts them in the back pages, if at all, which is okay with me," Hatch said rubbing his chin thoughtfully.

"Sounds about right."

"I think O'Leary's workin' the one yer askin' about, Frank."

"I'm doing a skip trace—old woman in Albina wants to find her missing son. Needs a general description of the guy, to rule him out, make sure it ain't her boy."

"Hey O'Leary? You got anything on that case? Frank here wants to know."

"Hold on a minute, I'm on the phone."

Dan O'Leary sat in a corner in the back of the office at a desk piled high with case files. With a head of curly grey hair, O'Leary was the stereotype of the paunchy old detective. He always wore suit pants that were too short, held up by suspenders that were two inches wide and generally bright yellow. His blue steel Colt .38 looked like an out of place toy gun, against his ample belly.

"You talkin' about that nigger kid shot in the back over on Commercial?" O'Leary asked, hanging up the phone.

"Yeah, is that *your* case, Dan?" Frank asked.

"No, and not much of a case either. Nothin' to go on. All I know is, the kid was shot in the back runnin' away. Probably got caught tryin' to steal somethin'. He took three in the back. Tight shot grouping. Three in the same spot. Took out most of the mid-spine, gone just like that. He didn't know what hit him. Probably dead before he hit the ground."

"Is that all there is, Dan?"

"Pretty sure that's it."

"Nobody heard shots or saw the shooter? I hear the other murders were about the same—shot in the back, robbed and left for dead on the street." The other detectives in the room looked at each other in turn with an intensity and wariness that was palpable and then looked back at Frank.

"Just curious is all. Funny how some things never change, huh?"

"You get outa here Frank!" Cunningham exploded, spittle flying, as he spat out the words.

Hatch looked over at him harshly, and once again everyone in the room ignored Cunningham. The other detectives maintained an intense interest in the conversation between Frank and Hatch. They were curious why an ex-street cop was asking questions about a string of murders in Albina. Was it really only because Frank was working a skip trace, or was there another reason? After standing for several minutes watching, Cunningham reached around and retrieved his fallen chair, sitting down on it, and staring at the floor while breathing hard.

"Yeah, that's all there is, Frank" Dan said.

"Okay, well thank you Dan. Appreciate it."

"No problem, Frank. I've been busy with a lot of other shit, lately. You know how it is. This guy wasn't the only one, though. Seems like every dumb fuck in this town is gettin' hisself kilt. Besides these four niggers that got blasted, I got two faggots in a house in Sellwood arguing over who was gonna suck whose dick. The loser wound up dead on the bedroom floor with a knife in his belly. Then there's been another "Bum-a-cide" to deal with! It never ends."

"Another one? Good Lord! Well, at least *that* hasn't changed" Frank laughed bitterly.

"Yep! Two wino's under the freeway ramp on the East side. Got into a drunken brawl over who knows what. One winds up dead down by the Willamette River and the other moron too drunk to remember what happened, or why." O'Leary finished his rant with a deep sigh and hefted his belt up, pushing his white shirt tail deeper into his pants.

"Sounds like you're shorthanded again, Dan. Just like the old days, huh?"

"You know it! We got over fifty homicides so far this year, Frank. We're so busy we're workin' cases alone, can't partner up anymore. The kid over on Commercial probably got what was coming to him. He should be identified in due course—maybe. And who knows about the others. Maybe *they* had it coming too?" Hatch paused to reflect a moment, looking over at the homicide blackboard crowded with comments, dates and names on the most recent murders.

"Cunningham over there is lookin' into the case of an old woman's skeleton found in an abandoned house off Hawthorne. Tryin' to figure out if she was murdered or just died of natural causes. I myself think it was murder, but that's just me."

"Well, thanks Dan. I appreciate the information."

"Anytime Frank, anytime."

Sergeant Blackburn stood staring out the window, gazing down on Third Street, the profile of his lined face visible. Frank hadn't noticed him and it took him a moment to remember him as he stood there, silent and motionless as a crow. Blackburn's left thumb was hooked inside his leather belt. His right hand fingered the holster containing a two inch .357 magnum snug against his right hip. He turned around with military precision, on his heel and stood facing Frank and his colleagues, stony faced. He'd been listening to the conversation and now he was seething. He glanced over to the chalk board, listing the most recent homicides, his eyebrows knit together in aggressive consternation. He stormed over to the board, angry; his shoulders raised and threw up his arm, pointing to the board.

"Do you know what this is?" he demanded, grabbing the eraser. No one spoke and Blackburn continued. "This one—and this one? And this one, and probably this fuckin' one right here, too?" he said pointing to the victims names.

"They're all dead jungle bunnies! All shot in the back. All runnin' away from the shooter." Blackburn looked at each detective in turn and then finally at Frank, waving the eraser in the air to make his point. "And when we knock on doors, no one heard any shots; no one saw anything and *no one* wants to talk to a cop!" Blackburn erased the top name so vigorously the chalk dust could be seen drifting up in languid spirals.

"And we cops are supposed to pretend we care—more than *they* care about their own people? The damned fuzzy headed spear-chucker's in *this* town cause most of the crime! And I'm supposed to jump up and give a shit when a few get whacked? And this guy?!" Blackburn said, pointing at Frank, "He ain't even a cop anymore and he's down here whinin' about a particular no good, trouble makin' thief that his poor Mama's looking for?"

"I'm workin' a skip trace, Blackburn! I gotta make a living."

"Yeah, right! Yeah, right!"

Blackburn strode over to the chalkboard and pounded the eraser on a nearby desk, bent over and in a rage, then threw it across the room where it landed with a thud against the wall. His face was red and the veins in his neck stood out like the veins in a race horses legs.

"That's it boys! The case is closed. Go to lunch!" Blackburn roared. He walked across the room, and stomped out the door, slamming it hard enough to rattle the glass and the frame.

"Yer done snoopin' McAllister! Get outa here!" Cunningham hissed. He leaned against the desk and adjusted his gun belt, trying to look menacing, shifting his considerable heft from foot to foot. "Just like Blackburn says. Get outa here now!"

Frank glanced over in Cunningham's direction, looking above his head and out the window in blissful disregard. His eyes were wide and his eyebrows raised, a small smile on his mouth. He searched his pockets for a cigarette, fishing out the wreck of a butt. He lit it slowly with his old Zippo, taking a deep luxurious drag, and blowing the smoke out at no one in particular. He turned the Zippo over in his hand and polished it on his jacket sleeve before pocketing it.

"Get out Frank!" Cunningham, hissed.

"Fuck off slick. Fuck off to both of ya! I'm a civilian now. I'm a free man."

"I'll have you arrested!"

"You're hallucinating. Arrest me for what?"

"I'll think a somethin!"

Frank laughed, slapping his thigh and leaning back on his heels. "You'll do nothing of the kind! I'm here, talkin' to a detective who also happens to be an old friend. And you're the same piece of shit you always were. Shut yer mouth you stupid reactionary!"

Cunningham stood behind his desk, seething, his chest rising and falling with each angry inhalation of breath. He glanced at Lt. Hatch who said nothing, just sat and smiled, amused at the proceedings.

Frank waved at Dan O'Leary, who sat at his desk, also smiling at the exchange, amused and utterly unmoved. The other detectives realized the show was over and begin dialing their phones and looking over their case files again. Frank reached over, giving Lt. Hatch's forearm a friendly squeeze.

"Let's go around the corner to Kelly's and have a few drinks, Hatch. I'll buy," Frank said.

"Sounds good, Frank. Hey it's good to see you, buddy. I'll be over in fifteen. And don't worry about Cunningham here; he's just going through another messy divorce. Isn't that right old buddy?"

This Ain't Working!

THE NEXT NIGHT was Frank's first night being Paladin. Theda dressed him in a sweat shirt with a hoodie, covered by an appropriately dark shabby overcoat rescued from a Goodwill bin. The look was completed with dark jeans and Frank's comfortable black running shoes. His .45 pistol rested comfortably in its holster on his right hip. With two extra loaded clips in his pocket, he felt relaxed and even a little excited to be back out on the street. It was kind of like being a cop again; something Frank missed more than he cared to admit. He was a hunter again but without a badge, which made things infinitely more complicated *and* risky.

Theda dropped him off near The Alibi on North Interstate, a popular tiki bar with cozy booths and a frequent meeting place for mixed race couples, safe from prying eyes. Frank decided he'd hang around the alley where patrons parked their cars and also stay close to the street in case Batman showed up. He walked back and forth lurching a little and acting unsteady on his feet, playing the part of a down and out drunk.

As Frank lurched by the open kitchen door in the alley, he breathed in the smell of fried chicken and remembered when he had worked the district and stopped by for their chicken and fries basket. How long had it been he wondered? Frank realized it was harder to act drunk than it was to actually *be* drunk and he hoped he looked the part. He was ready for something to happen. He was pumped. Maybe he should buy a piece of chicken first, though.

****

THEDA RETURNED TO her third floor apartment. She lit a joint on the fire escape just outside the apartment door, three stories above the big green dumpster. As the lid was usually open Theda often tossed her garbage sack over the fire escape railing and waited for the satisfying *thunk* when it hit dead center. To the west was the Willamette River, and nearby the ships that loaded grain at the grain-dock a few blocks away. Sometimes she could smell the wheat dust in the air and see the dust motes sparkle in the late afternoon sunlight as the pigeons flew back and forth feeding on fallen grain. To the east the Interstate five freeway to Seattle was heavy with traffic.

As Theda inhaled the smoke from the joint, she closed her eyes and soon the freeway sounds morphed imperceptibly into the sounds of the Oregon coast surf. She remembered one of only three times in her life she had ever been to the ocean. An outing she and some of her girlfriends from "Jeff" had planned, spending a weekend at Seaside and sleeping in the long station wagon she borrowed from her uncle. They built bonfires late at night beneath the dunes, giggling and talking about boys, their futures and all their plans. They hid behind the logs to avoid the blowing sand when it drifted into their beers and snuffed out their joints, and wrapped themselves in their mother's quilts brought along to keep them warm. They ate Ritz crackers, Cheese Whiz and fresh green grapes as they talked and laughed.

Theda wondered what happened to those girls who were having so much innocent fun all those years ago. She heard one of them traveled to Vegas with a boyfriend and disappeared into the night life, never to be seen again. Another flew to LA and disappeared there too. Theda remained in

Portland, tried college at Portland State for a year, but dropped out when she realized she wasn't ready to pick a major. After that she didn't know what she wanted to do, and she too slipped into the life. That meant running with Black Bart in St. Johns, staying out late, worrying her mother and wondering herself where she was headed and what might happen to her.

Now, with Batman on the loose and folks being murdered, the OG's wanted Theda's help in snaring Frank. She did what they wanted—they were family and would always be number one. But she felt a little guilty for sucking Frank in and now she realized she was worried about him being out there alone. Her thoughts were interrupted by Frank storming out of the elevator and striding in the open front door of the apartment.

"Where are you, Theda? This ain't workin'!'" he shouted. Theda stood up and carefully, stepped back in through the fire escape, and into the apartment. She stood looking Frank up and down; curious to see what was the matter. He seemed to be all right, but she could tell he was frustrated and angry.

"What happened? What's the matter big guy?"

"What's wrong is, I'm the only *white* guy within five fuckin' miles of the place. Even dressed like this I stick out like a sore thumb!"

"Frank, why do you smell like chicken?"

"The Alibi's back door was open. I was hungry."

"Well, if you were hungry, then why didn't you…"

"Theda, People are lookin' at me wondering what a white guy's doin' out that late and in that parta town. I look stupid! I can't be out here lookin' so damn white. You know, I'm probably just not the right guy for the job.

"Just take it easy, Frank."

"Yer not lookin' for Paladin—yer lookin' for John Shaft." Theda looked into Frank's face, deadpan, nodding her head reluctantly.

"Shaft wasn't available. Yer all we got!" she muttered, ignoring his rant.

She walked across the room and pulled her makeup bag from her purse, and walked back. She stood directly in front of Frank and helped him take off his overcoat.

"You'll have to do. Now, stand still and look directly above my head!" she ordered good naturedly. Theda began smoothing charcoal grey eye shadow across Frank's forehead, then under his eyes, working her way down, and blending it into his pale face. Frank stood uncomfortably, staring at the wall across the room with his hands dangling awkwardly at his sides. Theda took both his hands and placed them on her hips as she continued applying the dark eye shadow.

"Just relax, Sugar. I'm gonna make ya less noticeable is all."

Frank felt uncertain having his hands on Theda's hips. He could feel the outline of the braided leather belt she wore, tight at her small waist. But she felt good and smelled good too, there was no denying that. After only a few minutes, Theda stood back looking at Frank's new dark face shaking her head at what she saw.

"Are you making me black?" Frank asked, letting his hands drop from her hips, and trying not to smile in embarrassment.

"Well, it's more than color that makes ya black, Frank. Black is on the inside, too."

Theda sighed deeply, smiling at Frank. He felt he knew what she meant. It was a sigh that came from years of being a black woman and living in a white world, in white Portland, Oregon. It was a sigh of resignation, and frustration, and disgust.

Theda pulled out her make-up mirror, flipped it open and showed Frank his reflection. At first he frowned, he looked black but his eyes were still blue; bright blue. He pointed to his eyes with a comical look on his face, as if he were asking, *what about this?*

Theda realized what he meant and suddenly broke out laughing. Theda's laughter had a contagious quality to it and before he knew it, Frank saw the humor and began laughing, too. Together they laughed until Frank had to wipe tears from his eyes and Theda was gasping for breath. Frank walked to the bathroom to look in the big full-length mirror and bent over and laughed more, resting his hands on his thighs. It had been a long time since Frank had had a good hard laugh, and it felt good.

Batman

THE ROUTINE WAS *always the same. He woke up from his nighttime nap angry at not being able to find the crazy nigger who murdered his girlfriend Angela six years ago. The guy caught her walking home from work alone, headed to that dump NE apartment she was living in. He grabbed her purse and strangled her leaving her dead on the sidewalk like garbage. He'd tried to rape her but ran off before he could do it. When he took her money, he tossed her purse in the street. The one witness who saw him said the attacker was a "young black male" wearing a dark jacket and dark blue knit cap. The cops never found the guy, but Batman vowed he would find him—to kill him and leave him dead in the street, just like he'd left Angela. If he had to kill a dozen young black males in that part of town, Batman decided he would.*

Maybe tonight would be the last night he had to look. Maybe tonight he would find the right guy. He dressed in front of the large mirror. Donning black pants, a black turtle neck, a black ski-mask and a full length topcoat, with a hoodie jacket underneath, his .38 was strapped snugly to his hip. When he buttoned up his jacket, he scoffed at the reflection in the mirror.

"My own Mama wouldn't recognize me!" he murmured.

He didn't know of course that his victims called him Batman, but he would have loved the moniker; to be named after a superhero. With one last glance in the mirror Batman turned and walked down the narrow stairs to the garage. There it sat, gleaming, a 1969 black Cadillac, unlicensed and never out of the garage except at night.

The engine compartment had been specially muffled, the engine barely audible. It was his secret car. It only existed in darkness. He called it The Widow Maker. One switch turned off both the headlights and the tail lights at the same time, and another switch turned on the small police scanner mounted under the dashboard. It was a beauty and it got the job done. The job was robbing and killing and in Batman's mind, the only good "nignog" was a dead "nigog." He remembered his father saying so, all his life. The day would come when Batman would recognize Angela's killer, he knew that day would come. And if he killed enough of them he'd get the right one—and if he didn't so what? He'd killed a few already. There would be something in the right guys' eyes that would tell him. And when that recognition came, he'd put a bullet right between his eyes and there would be another dead nignog and so fuckin' what! He'd leave him dead in the street just like he left Angela. Just like that.

When he leveled his four inch barrel .38 at their bellies and ordered them to give up their money and their dope, he always hoped they'd bolt and run. That way he could shoot them like he did that one over on Commercial. They were usually too drunk to run, which made it easy, like knocking tin cans off the fence post. Batman reminded himself that street nignogs were only a "half a grade above a monkey," as his father always said. And only then because the nignogs could steal a car and monkeys couldn't. But one of them had killed Angela and someone was going to pay.

Too Drunk to Resist, Too Drunk to Run

FRANK LOOKED AT his watch. It was four thirty—the middle of the night. He had been out on the streets since just after one. It was cold. The kind of cold that settles in and chills everything till you can feel it deep in your bones. Roosevelt had loaned Frank a small flask, and filled it with Jack. He took a slug against the chill, wincing as it traveled down his throat, the wonderful burn helping him relax. He searched his pockets and found a crumpled cigarette in the bottom of the package. He found the old Zippo and lifted the top carefully because the hinge was coming off again. He would have to fix it and soon. He lit the cigarette, shrugged his shoulders against the night and continued his lurching stumble-walk, pretending to be drunk when he wasn't.

Frank was working the area around Roosevelt's after-hours club. He realized walking the streets and waiting to be robbed was keeping him hyper-aware and the stress showed in his clenched jaw and the way he felt the weight of his .45 hard against his body.

Frank was pretending to be drunk. He was pretending to be black. He was pretending to be a victim. But he was only *pretending*. Batman hadn't stopped robbing, but where was he and *who* was he? He hadn't killed anyone for a few weeks. How could Batman be in and out so fast, without anyone seeing? One night, a week after Frank started his nightly routine, Batman robbed a guy near the Alibi and Frank missed him. The next night it was, the Texas Playhouse. Two days after that, the long desolate alley behind Van's Olympic Room. It was a cat and mouse game Batman was playing, except that now Batman was the mouse, he just didn't know it.

They were legitimate night clubs, with bouncers and security. Batman didn't care which bar his victims came from just as long as they were good and drunk. Too drunk to resist and too drunk to run. Frank knew Batman had the perfect gimmick going for him, but it wouldn't last forever. The law of averages would work in Frank's favor, given enough time because that's how it always worked out; the law of averages always wins. After a fruitless night, Frank stumbled into Theda's apartment just as daylight was bringing a sparkle to the night dew. He fell across her bed, lying next to her, fully clothed. He was quietly snoring in less than two minutes. The dark charcoal eye shadow would have to come off later.

The Rising Cost of Smile Money

AFTER BREAKFAST WITH George at Dinty's, Charlie stood up, and hitched up his trousers, retying the tattered belt at his waist. He paid the ten dollar tab and left a five dollar tip for the waitress. He held the bill in his hand and smiled up at the waitress.

"Uh, you be sure and be extra nice to my friend George when I'm not in town." Then as almost an afterthought, he pointed at George.

"Very good man, George!" Charlie said. George smiled, embarrassed.

Charlie wheeled George out of the café and pushed him to the corner, waiting for the *walk* sign to come on.

"Uh, cross walks! Such bullshit!" Charlie mumbled to himself, smiling down at George. George clutched the paper cup of black coffee they left with, sniffed it, and took a sip.

"Yeah cross walks—didn't do my Alice any fuckin' good." George twisted in his wheel chair to get more comfortable. Charlie remained silent at the mention of Alice, the smile leaving his face as he pushed George across the street.

Arriving at the sidewalk elevator, they waited for the doors to open. Charlie pushed George inside and together they rode down to the basement of Mr. Lum's Chinese restaurant. Charlie was impatient at the progress of the slow moving freight elevator. He mumbled something unintelligible as it wobbled from side to side in its greasy rails finally stopping with a decided thunk. George rolled off and finding the light switch flooded the Blind Pig with yellowish light, which was fitting to the melancholy atmosphere of the slightly fetid basement room.

The Blind Pig was a collection of a dozen chairs or so that looked like they'd been salvaged from a local neighborhood dumpster. The bar was two 2 × 12 planks placed between two saw horses and sanded smooth on top. The planks were coated with clear varnish that was dotted with a constellation of cigarette burns of all shapes and sizes. Behind the bar was enough room for George to wheel himself about with ease. Beer was a dollar a bottle, either Millers or Pabst Blue Ribbon out of the case and was available to go if George knew a customer well enough.

The whiskey was Jack Daniels and Old Crow. Two dollars a shot and all profit as Mr. Lum furnished the booze except for the beer. George didn't sell soda pop or mixer, but for two bucks a shot and a dollar for a beer back, getting drunk was cheap. The basement of Mr. Lum's café smelled a little dank, but after an hour of serving alcohol, the cool-of-the-basement smell was not as noticeable and it became a sweet retreat of semi-darkness, cool temperatures and precious mind numbing booze. After George poured Charlie a double shot of Jack with a PBR back, he got himself a bottle of Miller beer and the two settled into drinks and conversation.

"Officer Arnie is coming by this morning to pick up his… ya know his weekly pay off?"

"Uh—how much this week?" Charlie asked.

"Oh, I don't know. He usually asks for the same amount.

Charlie slammed the double shot while breathing between his teeth, his jaw clenched, allowing the whiskey fumes to slowly escape his throat. A rustling at the top of the alley stairs let George know someone had pulled aside the pallets disguising the door and was coming down for a drink. Picking his way slowly down the narrow stairs, George could see officer Arnie waving his shiny billed police cap.

"Hey George! It's just me. Just old Arnie!"

Arnie was the day shift beat-cop out of Central Precinct. He'd been assigned this portion of the tenderloin for several years and enjoyed working it. Arnie knew everyone who lived in the area usually by their first names. If he didn't know you he made it his business to add you to his collection of mug shots. He was an old street cop and Arnie knew the score.

"Uh hello officer," said Charlie, turning his head away so as to spare Arnie the alcohol fumes.

"I didn't know you were in town Charlie. Haven't seen you in jail for awhile!"

"Uh, didn't like yer accommodations last time," said Charlie taking a sip of his PBR and smiling good naturedly.

"Gotta talk to ya George," Arnie said reaching over and helping himself to a Miller beer. He pulled off the cap with a key chain bottle opener he fished out of his pocket.

"I'm gettin' a lot a heat down at the precinct. The liquor dicks are hangin' round asking all kinds of questions. They hear there's an unlicensed establishment somewhere around here. They say it's probably on my beat and as I'm the beat cop, I'm supposed to know what the fucks goin' on." Arnie chuckled to himself. "Like I don't know what's goin' on? Course I do."

"George, everyone that's doin' business on the down side— ya know like *you?* Well, they gotta pay the tariff. Legit places pay the city; the other guys in this part of town pay *me.* I've been easy on ya with only a hundred a week, but with all the attention I gotta raise my prices. It'll have to be a hundred fifty a week startin' next week. Then I got absolutely no idea what the OLCC guys are talkin' about, okay?" The three men were silent for a moment and George poured Charlie another double shot.

"Uh, I'll help pay for it George? Don't you worry none. I'll have the money next week." Charlie felt a scowl pass over his face as he turned slightly in his chair to avoid eye contact with Arnie. "Don't worry you'll be ok. I'll take care of the difference. George, he's my friend." Arnie shrugged twirling his shiny billed police cap on his trigger finger.

"I don't care where it come from as long as it winds up in *my* pocket. Gotta get as much as I can *while* I can ya know? Cause a retired cop don't get tuh make the rounds no more. And that's coming up, soon. I gotta take care of *me* you know?" Arnie finished his beer and put the empty bottle back in the case.

"You want another, Arnie?" offered George.

"Nah, I gotta get back to the street. This is collection day for a couple of places. My next stop is the Hamilton. A couple small time smack dealers on the second floor owe me money. I'm not too hard on them, but they better be payin' up. They kinda keep the neighborhood straight ya know? Supply the junkies with the meds they need for the day. Helps me out, cause then I know where most of em' are! They're sleepin' and noddin' out somewhere. Funny, how some things never change."

"I remember them!" George chimed in.

"My Alice and I used to live on the third floor...before... well ya know before that day. There's a pot dealer there, too. I used to watch him bring in a paper shopping bag filled with two finger-lids every few days. But strong alcohol is the only thing that helps the pain in *my* damn back." George twisted again moving slightly forward in his wheel chair to relieve the ever present pressure in his mid-back. Charlie frowned but said nothing as he watched George squirm uncomfortably in his chair, trying to get relief.

The last George and Charlie saw of officer Arnie was his ample rump moving up the narrow stairs covered by his shiny-in-the-butt blue twill police trousers. The door closed and once again they were alone. George shook his head knowing that an additional fifty a week for Arnie meant he would have to stay open longer and serve more customers. That meant more risk of the wrong people finding out about The Blind Pig.

"I hope Arnie can protect me, Charlie." Charlie patted George on the back and helped himself to another PBR.

"Uh, don't worry. I have to take the bus back to the rez tonight, but I'll be back in a few days when I get my check. I'll pay Arnie. Don't you worry George."

"I sure do appreciate that Charlie. I don't know why you're bein' so good to me, but I sure can use the help."

An hour and twenty minutes into the Greyhound ride back to the Warm Springs Reservation Charlie could see the landscape slowly change outside the tinted window as they traveled up the Mt. Hood highway. The tall stands of Douglas Fir gave way to the sparse and spindly evergreen growth and sagebrush that covered the landscape. As the bus stopped at the *Kahneeta Resort* entrance road and Charlie breathed in the smell of pine, he knew he was home again, and could somehow breathe a little easier.

It was seven and one half miles up hill from the bus stop to the wooden shack Charlie called home. He would hitchhike; he always did, and walk halfway there or all the way there. It would be okay. But as Charlie lurched along the road, a tired figure leaning to the right, he wrestled with an awful secret bundled up inside his troubled mind. With every step he took the burden grew heavier, like a dark arrow in his soul covering a festering wound that refused to heal.

Back to the Office

FRANK UNLOCKED THE door to room ten, his "office" at the Lotus. The mail delivered through the mail slot had collected and the bulk of the pile blocked the door. He pushed hard, squeezed in, bent over and gathered it up, placing it on top of the dusty desk. He sorted through the junk mail, pizza coupons and "get your oil changed" certificates and set aside a few bills. There was a note from Midge that his rent was overdue. He pushed the play button on his answering machine, and listened to several messages and was surprised at all the work that was piling up. The bank had cars they needed repossessed, and an insurance company wanted him to find out if a certain person named on a policy was really deceased or living under an assumed name collecting welfare in the North End. He made notes on the fresh yellow pad retrieved from the inside of his desk drawer and sat down on the couch, looking around his office.

Frank hadn't slept in room ten for almost two weeks, and the place smelled musty. The old office didn't seem as comfortable and looking at the note pad and the work piling up he realized how absorbed he was in catching Batman. He made the necessary calls to the bank and the insurance company. Promising to get back to them if he got someone on the phone and leaving messages if he didn't.

He tore off the top sheet of the yellow pad, tri-folded it and stuffed it in his pocket and then locked up, leaving the table lamp on so the other tenants wouldn't think his place was empty. He walked down the dim hall on the ultra thick carpeting that made each step as silent as a ninja's. He stepped into the darkened side entrance staircase, feeling the unmistakable feeling he always felt there, that he was being watched. The Lotus had its secrets and he wondered if the stories about ghosts were true. He knew people had died in the rooms and not just one or two, but in fact several. And he knew about the notorious basement ghost and the cold chill employees reported feeling when they went down to collect food and supplies.

He walked into the bar downstairs, picked the end stool and plopped down in front of Midge looking over at her tiredly. "Long time no see Frank. Where ya been stayin? You shacked up with that—that woman?" Frank noted the sarcasm in her voice, and felt he was being scolded.

"Theda—her name is Theda, and can I get a Bloody Mary without getting the third degree?" He opened his wallet to pay for the drink and laid out the rent money, a neat pile of twenties on top of the bar.

"This is for the rent, too."

"That'll cover it."

Midge set down the drink and scooped up the rent money, putting it in the till and reaching for the receipt book. Grabbing a bar towel, she leaned over Frank, mopping up a little tomato juice.

"What have ya been up to Frank? This bar is goin' broke since ya don't do yer drinkin' here no more."

"I'm just workin' Midge, tryin' to catch a murderin' thief. It's takin' a lot of time, but I'm okay. Been drinkin' in the hood, ya know, Albina? That garbage dump neighborhood of crud and corruption where I used to work when I was a cop?"

"Oh yeah, I remember that place. Seems I used to live there once as well." Frank found his cigarettes in his shirt pocket and tried to light a cigarette, but the hinge broke and the top came off, dropping loudly to the wood bar top.

"Dammit. Midge, you got a paper clip back there somewhere? This thing's broke again. By the way, who were those two suits I saw leaving when I came in? I didn't recognize them as cops. You know who they are?" Midge turned around and fished around in a big dusty glass jar behind the cash register. It was filled with pencils, rubber bands, paper clips and other odds and ends.

"Oh, them guys? They were just a couple of liquor dicks. They said they heard about an unlicensed establishment around here and wanted to know if I knew anythin' about it." She delivered the requested paper clip, looking down at the broken Zippo on the bar with a frown.

"But I stiffed 'em."

"Good. We don't need any trouble here."

"Frank, ya know they fix those things for free if you send em' back to the factory." Frank twisted another piece of thin paper clip wire until it broke off and inserted the new piece into the hinge. He flicked the Zippo, lit the Marlboro, and blew smoke in Midges direction, an impish smile on his face. He turned the battered old lighter over in his hand, looking at it, feeling the metal and polished it on his pant leg.

"Nah, it wouldn't be the same. I'll keep fixin' this one until it can't be fixed anymore."

"Or you could just quit smoking?"

"Yep, I could do that, too," he responded.

"Why doncha, Frank?"

"I'll quit smokin' when I can't fix this lighter anymore. That's when I'll quit." He polished the lighter again, pressing it against his shirt front and returned it to his pocket.

"Ya still workin' for gangsters?"

"They're not really gangsters like ya think."

"You said they were gangsters. You called em' OG's.

"Think of OG's as a term of endearment. Kinda like old grandpa."

"So now yer workin' for some old grandpa's? Yer not makin' sense Frank. I hope you don't get into any trouble. I consider you a friend, you know?"

"I know Midge, and I appreciate that. I do." Frank said. He slammed down the rest of his Bloody Mary, took the remaining celery stick with him to chew on and left a five dollar bill on the bar, waving goodbye to Midge as she began serving another customer. Frank walked out of the Lotus and into the bright light of Third Avenue just in time to see George emerge from the sidewalk freight elevator. They nodded in recognition but said nothing. Frank knew The Blind Pig would be a secret from the OLCC yet another day.

Theda as Frank's Back-Up

FRANK, I GOTTA go with you and be yer back up!"

"I dunno about that."

Theda was nearly finished with their nightly ritual of applying the dark eye shadow on Frank's face. He laughed and backed out of her reach slightly.

"Being out in the streets in the middle of the night is not where *you're* supposed to be. Besides, you're just a girl. You need to stay out of harm's way." Theda placed her hands on his shoulders, pulled him back within range and continued putting on the dark make up. She was smiling as she smoothed it on with the makeup sponge.

"So, I'm just a girl huh? I can't stay here in this little apartment smokin' joints and worryin' myself sick about you. You need back-up!" Theda said firmly, punctuating her speech by flicking specks of dandruff off Frank's shoulder.

"Theda, you know what I mean. I don't want you getting hurt. If you're a block away as my backup, then you're just a victim yourself. What if Batman picks on you again like he did at Van's. He might recognize you. Then not only do I have to take care of myself, I have *you* to protect, too. Nope, it's too dangerous. It's just no place for a woman."

"Then-I'll-be-out-there-anyway-and-you-won't-see-me-until-you-need-me!"

"Theda?!"

"And, besides Mr. Neon loaned me a .38. Remember, this is *my* neighborhood! I know all the back alleys, trust me." Theda stared at Frank, her amber eyes sparkling, daring him to contradict her.

"Honey? What makes you think I don't know every back alley, too?" Theda looked down embarrassed.

Frank shook his head and took a deep breath, exhaling slowly. He could see Theda was determined and he wouldn't be able to stop her short of tying her up. And there was something about Theda that was compelling and confident. Frank *knew* he could trust her.

"Okay!" she said, as if the matter was settled.

"Okay, what?"

"Tonight we should work around Mr. Neon's place up on NE 14th and Killingsworth. It's not as fancy as Roosevelt's with the draperies and near-to-new poker tables; it's more of a workin' man's place. The entry door is off the old driveway at the side of the house. It's rundown and looks like nobody lives there and there's even a *For Sale* sign in the window."

"And?"

"Most of the folks who go there at night go to drink beer and play poker, smoke a little pot, and hang out. A lot of black city workers go there, ya know? The guys who work at Stanton Yard? Water Bureau guys, road pavin' guys, they go there, too."

"Is that right? Why am I not surprised?"

"They have a weekly poker tournament. Good crowd, just plain folks. They're not crooks Frank. Course Mr. Neon keeps up the insurance on the place. He says when he's tired of runnin' an after-hours; it'll catch fire or something!" Theda and Frank both smiled, not surprised that Neon Jones had a backup plan for his after-hours business—in the event of it going out of business.

Attraction and Conflict

THEDA: SHE STOOD in the darkness away from the streetlight a block east on Killingsworth and shifted from foot to foot so she could keep Frank in view. He looked good, like any other drunk black guy trying to figure out which way was home. She could tell the way he lurched and swayed, he'd been drunk a few times in his life. People were parking their cars on the neighborhood side streets and quietly walking up the crumbling driveway of the old beat up house with the *For Sale* sign in the window. The people were all conspicuously silent. Some were arriving and some were leaving and some drove by slowly to see if Neon's place was open.

No one stopped to talk to Frank. He was a slouchy black man they didn't recognize, with squinty eyes who wouldn't look at them. Theda pulled her warm coat over her chest, and checked to see that the loaded .38 was secure in her pocket. It felt good and she felt safe. It was Frank she was worried about. Theda realized she had become fond of Frank in spite of herself. He was easy going, amiable, and it seemed to happen all on its own, this growing fondness morphing into something deeper.

Sometimes Theda looked at him while he was sleeping with his mouth slightly parted, his eyes closed and his face so relaxed and innocent looking she felt a tender fondness growing. He was so damned *white,* though! But he was different from the other three white men she'd been with. They were the kind of guys who took her to dinner and then wanted to fuck her right away, thinking she would of course, since she was black. They were the kind of guys who thought they were cool walking with a pretty black woman on their arms, a woman so skinny that her friends used to call her Skinny Minnie. But they were shallow guys, party guys. They were the kind of white men the old folks sometimes called "blue eyed devils."

Theda remembered hearing that all her life from her own family. White folks were "blue eyed devils," and nothing more. Somehow she knew that was wrong, too, because she felt safe with Frank. He was laid-back but strong and she knew he'd never run on her. Theda knew he was not the cynical hard-ass he pretended to be, but she also knew he was tough enough to handle himself. And he hadn't once made a pass at her though they were together day and night. Theda was intrigued and could no longer deny that. She was beginning to feel she didn't *want* Frank to go back to his office and be a PI anymore. She was conflicted as she watched him stumble around pretending to be drunk. Theda didn't want Frank to go back to his old work. She wanted something *with* him, she didn't know what. And of course there was the troublesome fact that he was white.

Frank: As Frank looked up Killingsworth Street where Theda was hovering, he could barely make out her dim outline in the shadows. This little girl was just up the street packin' a gun that her fine-boned elegant hand could barely hold. Never in a million years could he imagine himself in this situation. Maybe she could be his secretary, and help out in the office? He wondered if she could type and then decided it didn't matter. The typewriter was rarely used, anyway. Frank just wanted her around. Maybe she could help out at the office, but how could he suggest it without coming across as forward?

Frank was tired of stumbling around pretending to be drunk, pretending to be a victim. On the other hand he knew that *the law* was on his side. The law of averages, that is.

As long as Batman kept coming out at night and robbing and shooting, eventually it would be Frank's turn to bump into him. He lit a Marlboro and flashed his lighter to signal Theda. Batman would not get caught this night and it was time to go home. She nodded her head briefly and began walking away, in the opposite direction, toward Frank's car.

Black Bart Returns

THE POUNDING AT Theda's apartment door was insistent, getting louder as the door went unanswered. Frank dozed, lying across Theda's pull down bed—his long legs sprawled over the side. Theda was in the bathroom steaming the wrinkles out of Franks pants, wrinkled from stumbling around outside of Roosevelt's after-hours all night. They were weary and disappointed.

"Somebody's at the door, Theda!"

"Answer it!"

"But I don't have any pants on."

"Throw on my old robe. It's on the end of the couch."

Frank looked at the robe, old beige chenille, with oversized red and yellow flowers, and three sizes too small for him. He shrugged and frowned, and threw the robe over his shoulders tying it closed around his lean waist. His bare legs were showing from mid-thigh down and he still had some of the black make up in the wrinkles on his forehead, around his eyes and in the creases of his neck. He looked a little like Lurch, from *The Adams Family* TV show, or a drunken Thespian too lazy to remove all the stage make-up after a long and grueling performance of Othello.

Frank knew he looked ridiculous but he answered the door anyway, slowly pulling it open. The face staring at him was older, with fuller cheeks than he remembered, and an emerging double chin. The almost black eyes were so dark they were nearly maroon and still as threatening as before with bushy eyebrows furrowed together in a familiar expression of consternation and aggression. When the man spoke he showed yellowed teeth which were probably part of the reason the breath emanating from his mouth was so offensive. The face at the door slowly morphed into a mug shot stored in Frank's memory. It was *Bartholomew Williams*, aka Black Bart. The same Black Bart who had been a thief and heroin dealer, the man in charge of most of the crime in the St. Johns district all during the wild 1960s.

St. Johns was a crime ridden ghetto back then. Downtown St. Johns sat to the north of the foot of the St. Johns Bridge that crossed west into Linnton, a lumber mill-town, and another hard drinking village. City politicians thought so little of St. Johns they considered it a suitable location for the city dump. In the summer when a high breeze was blowing you could tell from the smell carried on the wind, just exactly where the dump was located.

Frank remembered Black Bart was involved in a shootout in the alley behind the Wishing Well tavern. He'd killed another dope dealer. Bart called it self-defense. The DA called it manslaughter and gave Bart ten to fifteen. Frank remembered Bart alright. He was trouble and a face a cop or former cop wouldn't soon forget.

"Hey man, I'm lookin' for T, my old girl! Theda? I heard she move here."

Frank made no effort to move out of the way as Bart looked from left to right, trying to see around Frank and into the apartment. He appeared to have no memory of Frank as he looked from side to side. After a moment, Theda walked tentatively out of the bathroom, a clean white towel wrapped around her waist and wearing a pink push-up bra. Her silky brown shoulders gleamed in the light and her breasts stood up like tin solders standing at attention. The sight of Theda in her hot-pink bra and towel was riveting.

Bart's demeanor changed as soon as he saw Theda. His face fell and the expression of simple curiosity changed to a look of longing and pained recognition. This was the woman he had loved and lost—the one he had waited for. This was the woman he hoped would be there for him upon his release. Theda stood there, still stunning, with youth, health and time all on her side, but her eyes were wide and she looked afraid. It had been almost a decade since she'd seen Bart.

"Hey T, is that you? Told ya I'd be out soon. Sent ya some letters? Never did hear back from ya. Eight long years, baby—eight long years?" There was a long silence and then Theda spoke.

"That was a long time ago, Bart. Things are different now. We can't go back to the past." Theda walked over and stood behind Frank as she tightened the towel around her waist.

"Come on baby, let's smoke a little weed. We can listen to some tunes, like old times?"

"Bart, that was all so long ago. Things have changed."

"Aww, come on baby? It's me? Bart! It's me, baby!"

"Bart, you need to go. We can't go back to how it was. That time is over."

Frank pumped up his aura and worked his face into a scowl made more menacing with the left over makeup and his crazy appearance in a woman's flowered bathrobe.

"The lady said you should leave, now."

"Please leave Bart?" Bart's sincere expression and pleading tone disappeared. His face erupted into a grin and he started laughing, slapping his hands together.

"Oh, I see how it is, baby!" he said moving back a step

"This must be the landlord. You must be payin' the rent, huh baby girl?"

"Oh, Bart."

"If'n ya need help payin' the rent T, jus lemme know. I'll help ya out. We can *negotiate* on it." Bart turned his back, still intent on convincing Theda and Frank they were a big joke, but his forced laughter contained the unmistakable timbre of despair. Instead of walking to the elevator, Bart jogged to the fire escape just to the left of the apartment front door and with forced bravado, easily climbed down to the first floor, jumping the last few feet to the ground. He looked up to see if Theda had noticed, but she wasn't standing there. She stood frozen in the living room, the look of fear still on her face.

"See ya T," Bart said quietly, with a wave to no one. "I'll be around, baby. Eight long years. Eight long years, gone."

Theda Talks about Her Past

MAKING SURE BART was on the ground and had left Frank closed the door to the apartment, and walked to the couch. He sat down; making sure the too-small robe covered his groin.

"Looks like your boyfriend wants ya back, huh?"

"My boyfriend?"

Theda walked to the closet next to the kitchen, reached up and began to rummage through a small shoe box. She retrieved a bundle of letters tied together with a tattered light blue satin ribbon and tossed them at Frank. He caught the bundle midair and tried not to notice that the towel around her waist was becoming loose and wasn't secured. He saw her slender brown legs and a glimpse of matching hot-pink panties as she sat on the edge of the bed next to him.

"He wrote me a lot of letters from the joint in Salem. They're all there. Go ahead and read them if ya want. I never answered *any* of them. Not one. He has no reason to think I was waiting for him to get outa jail! Can't believe he showed up like that. Fuck! He didn't even ring the front door buzzer; just climbed up the fire escape! He used to do stuff like that in the old days. Liked to brag about how he could climb up or down any fire escape in less than a minute."

"Impressive!" Frank said blandly.

"Poor, old Bart. He's still the same angry fool tryin' to impress me. Actin' tough, actin' a fool." Theda leaned back on the bed and smoothed out the towel covering her legs.

"What do you wanna do? He'll be back you know."

"It was all so long ago I hardly remember it." Theda nervously lit a joint and lay flat on the bed, crossing her long legs and blowing smoke at the ceiling. Frank turned to watch her, and realized he was jealous at the arrival of Bart. But he felt protective, too. Bart was a lot older than Theda and clearly damaged goods.

"Do you mind my asking how old you were, when you guys got together?"

"I was nineteen when I met Bart. He was good lookin' then. Smooth, you know, pretty? He had nice teeth and he had money, including a pimped out black Mercury Marquis with deep dish chrome wheels, white pin-striping and maroon leather seats with a diamond pattern in the back. You remember the kind?"

"Sure, I do."

"I knew he was a heroin dealer *and* a pimp but I got stuck on him for a while. In some ways, Bart knew how to treat a woman. We were together for a couple a years off and on. He kept trying to get me to use heroin and be one of his girls." Theda lit the joint again and took another hit. The blue smoke drifted to the ceiling in thin, delicate tendrils.

"But I was too smart for that shit. I saw what happened to the other girls he had workin' for him. Despite him tellin' me I was the best thing that ever happened to him, he couldn't stop that urge to wanna turn me out. It was in his blood. He was a pimp all the way though. And he was mean, too. He beat on them; some of them girls weren't even fifteen." Theda sat silent for a minute smoking the joint and studying her fingernails.

"Besides, I wanted to go to college!" Theda announced, looking at Frank with wide owlish eyes. The expression on her face was equal parts innocence and cynicism, and heartbreaking in its way.

"I wanted to get me some of that *education!* You know, more than only Jeff? I wanted to go all the way to Portland State University!"

"Did you like it?"

"It was okay. And I got good grades, too! For a while anyway." Theda stopped, looking down and toying with an opal and silver ring on her wedding finger.

"What happened?"

"I don't know. All those white kids? They weren't very welcoming. The girls all felt threatened by me. I was prettier than most of em' and too many of the white boys just wanted to see what it would be like to bed down with some brown sugar. That's what they used to call us black girls, thinkin' it was cute. Brown Sugar!"

"I know the type."

"I lasted a bit over a year, then I just stopped going to class. I did my year. I proved I could do it. My mama was so proud, lemme tell you! Told all her friends I graduated. God, poor Mama."

"Did Bart want you to drop out?"

"He was so crazy; he couldn't even remember I was a student half the time. Then he started drinkin' Hennessey straight from the bottle. Made him even meaner. His other rival in the St. Johns smack business was a niggah named Hizetis, I forget his last name. Goodsmith maybe, somethin' like that. Bart was gonna kill him and take over his business. Had it all planned out."

"I came up against the Hizetis brothers a few times. I recall the name." Frank maneuvered into a more comfortable position on the couch, and continued listening.

"Bart caught Hizetis drinkin' in the Wishing Well out on Lombard one night. He waited till he left out the back door, to the alley? Then Bart pulled out his .38 and confronted him, but Hizetis saw him coming and fired the first shot, cause he was packin' too of course. Bart got lucky when Hizetis missed and then Bart shot him in the throat. Killed him but it took a while for him to bleed out. You know how a shot like that is?"

"I do indeed."

"Bart walked across the alley, towards where Hizetis was layin, and fired two more shots to make sure he was dead." Theda stopped for a minute and then continued—her eyes wide and haunted.

"That's what fucked up his defense. Cause Hizetis fired the first shot, Bart claimed self-defense, but the DA prosecuted Bart anyway, cause he fired two more shots to make sure Hizetis was dead."

"I remember hearing about the case. It was long after I left the bureau of course."

"He wanted to give him the *acuda-gra* and he sure did. They put Bart in prison and I ain't seen him since. Not until now. He's mean and dangerous, Frank. He can't listen to reason and he's stupid. Ghetto stupid. I'm afraid, now that he's back. I won't lie, I'm afraid!"

"Okay. But I'm *not* afraid of him, Theda. Two .45 slugs in his belly and what's left of him'll be cryin' for his mama. Don't worry honey, I'm not gonna let anything happen to you."

"Thanks Frank. *Really!* Cause I know you didn't ask for any-a-this."

"It's okay. Everything will work out, it always does."

"Everything works out?"

"Sure, honey. In one way or another."

Frank looked up as Theda rose to her feet and covered him with the soft flannel blanket resting on the end of the couch. Her pretty smiling face was the last thing he saw before he closed his eyes. She tucked him in all the way around, smoothing back the grey curl that fell over his forehead, and then walked tiredly to the pull-down Murphy bed with the towel still wrapped around her waist. Theda lay across the bed and pulled the quilt over her, turning to face the wall and curling up.

"Goodnight Frank. I'll make us an omelet tomorrow, okay?"

"Sounds good—guh-night Theda."

If Bart had been outside the door, he would have heard them both breathing quietly in the gathering purple shadows, the city lights outside the apartment slowly dimming. Frank was nearly asleep when he calculated Theda's age. She was nineteen when she met Bart, and hung with him for a couple of years. Bart being in prison for eight years made Theda only about twenty nine. He considered how young she still was, and how lucky she'd been able to get away from Bart. No, nothing would happen to Theda. Frank would make certain of that.

Roosevelt's Advice

BART STOOD SWAYING—A mostly empty pint of Hennessey's gripped in his right hand. His black sport jacket was askew and his black turtle neck sweater wet from spilling some down the front.

"I need to talk to ya, Roosevelt!" Bart slurred.

The door to the back room of the Burger Barn framed the slight figure of the elderly waitress, Miss Raiford. She was shaking her head, her shoulders raised in fright.

"I told him you men was busy, but he wouldn't listen!" Roosevelt stood up abruptly at seeing Bart and reached inside his belt, pulling out his .38. He calmly placed the gun on the table in front of him. Neon Jones stood too, laying down a deck of cards and taking a step away from the table, his eyes alarmed.

"We heard y'all was back in town, Bart," said Neon carefully.

"That's right. I'm back!"

"Can I say it's good to see ya?" said Neon, glancing over at Roosevelt.

Roosevelt kept his hand near the pistol and a frown plastered on his face. His shrewd brown eyes took in the scene in front of him. The white fringe of short hair set off his shiny bald head as he watched Bart, keenly aware of the potential for serious trouble.

Bart lurched forward and slumped into a chair. Neon and Roosevelt looked at each other meaningfully and as Bart sat down, they did too. Bart slugged down the last of the alcohol, gulping it noisily and belching loudly, and laid the empty on the table. Still, Roosevelt kept his eye on his .38 while he watched Bart's every move.

"Need my shit back!" mumbled Bart, nodding his head affirmatively.

"Gotta get back in business. Need some cash. Need my girl, Theda!" Roosevelt spoke slowly; making sure Bart understood every word.

"Ya been gone a long time Bartholomew. Eight years. Nothing's the same. It's changed."

"I want ma territory back! I want St. Johns. Fuck all this 'things is changed' shit. I'm back!"

"Even if we could, it ain't in our power to do nothin' anymo." Roosevelt lowered his voice to a whisper before continuing.

"Most of the dope business is run by da cops, now anyways. Maybe two no-account Mexicans is still workin' out there but the cops is either workin' with 'em or..." Roosevelt left the thought unfinished.

"What fuckin' Mexicans? I knew some Mexicans in the joint. They can't fight. They SOFT!"

"The Longorias, Dominic and his brother Enrique. They must have somethin' goin' with the cops. Most of the gangstas are out in St. Johns now, Albina's pretty quiet. Except for Batman. Ya heard he murdered my grandson Jojo didn't ya?"

"Hears sumpin' bout it. Hears ya hired a white guy tuh get 'em. None of the brother's tough enough to take care of this so called Batman? That why ya hired a paddy white dude?"

"Sometimes Bartholomew," said Roosevelt still speaking slowly, "the right person comes along for the job. And sometimes the right person does the right thing, and when that happens the color of they skin jus' don't matter much."

"Yeah, right! Color matter Mr. Roosevelt. Color always matter!"

"Yes, it do Bart. Yes, it do."

"And you can't get someone else tuh take care of this—this batman?" Bart demanded.

"Batman is a murdering, robbing thief takin' advantage of drunk niggah's late at night, Bart! When they too drunk tuh fight back. Jojo musta tried tuh runaway. Batman shot him in the back. Turned his pockets inside out, picked his wallet clean and left ma boy dead on the street, with his hand palm deep in gutter water. Cops won't do nuthin' bout it. They say they don't know who shot Jojo. But they ain't lookin' neether. Everybody knows they don't care bout colored folks. They only care bout theirselves."

"This ain't news to ME!" said Bart.

"That's why we hired Frank McAllister," said Neon, calmly.

"Some white paddy who used tuh be a cop!"

"He called himself Paladin. He was jokin' Bart. He a straight shooter, that one—Frank got a heart."

"I remember Paladin," said Bart suddenly growing thoughtful.

"We watched the re-runs in the joint, and back when I was a kid, too." Suddenly Bart stood up and placed his hands on the poker table and sucked in a deep breath.

"Well, let me re-introduce ma-sef. This is the niggah *Bart-man*. I'll get this Batman for ya inna cuppa days. Ya can send Paladin home. T, she'll come home to Bart then, too. Jes watch, it's gonna happen."

Bart turned and staggered out the back door leaving his empty Hennessey bottle on the poker table. Roosevelt tucked the .38 back in his belt, and the two men looked at each other, both taking deep breaths and looking out the window at Bart's disappearing, bobbing head, bent forward and slumping down the darkened street.

"Might be trouble," said Neon, as Bart disappeared, heading north. Roosevelt just shook his head and retrieved a can of Old English from the fridge behind him, popped the top and took a long swig. Then he picked up the deck of cards and shuffled them and began dealing.

"My money's on Paladin, Mr. Jones. My money's on that ole' fired cop."

On The Sidewalk Looking up

BART STOOD ON the sidewalk in front of Cadillac Candy's after-hours joint swaying a little in the darkness and shaking his whiskey flask to see how much Hennessey's he had left. Satisfied there were a couple swigs remaining he lifted it and emptied it, wiping his mouth on his sleeve. Bart was drunk. He made a big production of delicately screwing on the cap, and returning the flask to his hip pocket. He stood looking up and down the street slowly becoming aware of his surroundings. The hour was late but he was not the only person on the sidewalk.

Looking around Bart noticed the figure of a woman in a long black overcoat. The street light illuminated her enough so he could see the coat was tied at the waist with one end of the belt hanging lower than the other. Bart swayed towards her. She heard someone approaching and turned to face him. As he staggered closer the woman recognized him.

"Theda baby, you're waiting for me? I knew ya would girl. Musta seen me goin' in an hour ago. Sure, that's it. Come on; let's go to your place and party. Ya got any smoke?" Bart, all smiles now, reached over and tried to put his arm around Theda's shoulders, but she pushed him off. He leaned in and pulled her to him, and began nudging her up the street, smiling and laughing as if they were playing a game. Theda pulled out of his grasp, becoming angry.

"I'm not waitin' on you! Leave me alone! Get off me!" Bart stepped back, staggered, but caught himself.

"What's wrong witcha baby? Les go party. Hey, it's me, Bart. What you doin' out here if you not waitin' on old Bart?"

"I'm waitin' on someone else, a friend, that's all."

"Come onnnn, Theda!" Bart said, feeling suddenly powerful from the alcohol, "Let's play!" Bart grabbed Theda by the shoulder, getting a handful of her coat in his fist, moved his hand up her neck and grabbed her by the hair, mussing it.

"You stop it, Bart!"

Frank heard Theda shouting up the street and squinted his eyes to better see her. She was struggling with a man. Frank recognized the man as Bart and closed the distance between them sprinting down the street in less than a minute.

"He's tryin' to get me to go home with him, Frank! I won't! I won't do it!"

"Okay, back off Bart! Back off, now!"

"Git yer damn hands off me, Bart!" Bart wheeled to face Theda's protector, but once again, almost fell.

"You leave that little girl alone, you damn filthy bastard!" Frank said through his teeth.

Frank pulled Theda out of Bart's reach, pushing her firmly behind him. Bart steadied himself and tried for a left hook but he swung too hard and too wide, and nearly fell over. Frank knew a man as powerful as Bart might be more than he could handle, *if* he was sober, but Bart wasn't sober, he was drunk, stumbling, falling down drunk.

Frank gripped Bart by the back of his jacket, and pulled hard, to throw him off balance, but Bart came back at him. Frank grabbed his jacket at the shoulders, filling each fist with fabric, gaining leverage, and pushed him backwards onto the sidewalk, where he landed flat on his back. Bart sat up, surprised for a moment, and reached down into his shoe and pulled something out. Then Bart seemed to propel upwards as if an unseen force was lifting him. As he stood across from Frank, there was a gleaming straight razor gripped tightly in his hand, the silver blade glinting. Frank pulled his .45 from the holster on his hip, and pointed it flush at Bart's face.

"Try it stupid!" Frank spat in an angry whisper. They were both breathing hard as Frank cocked the .45 ominously, but the familiar click made Bart stop, razor in hand, uncertain.

"You'll be a blood puddle on the sidewalk surrounded by the bone splinters of what *used* to be yer fuckin' head, Bart!"

"Okay, take it easy, pinkie! Take it easy!"

"Shut yer mouth and get the fuck outa here! Now!"

Bart stared into Frank's blue eyes and then at the big hole at the end of the gun as Frank took a step forward, pushing the barrel closer, but keeping a safe distance. It was then Bart had a rare moment of clarity. He deliberately backed away and stood, still swaying, calculating his next move.

"Don't worry T, I'll get that Batman everyone talkin' bout."

"Bart, you just go home now, okay?" Theda said in quiet desperation.

Bart staggered away confused by what had just happened. Who was that guy with Theda? Was he really a black guy with blue eyes? How could *that* be? Soon Bart could be heard laughing, as he ambled away on unsteady feet.

"Blue eyes?" he asked no one in particular as he continued to walk away.

"Mus be the landlord, yeah, the landlord. I'll jes get rid of em, *my* way! And I'll have my St. Johns back in jusa few days' time. Theda'll come back to old Bart, then. She not gonna stay with some no-dick white paddy motherfucker. She'll want old Bart back, just like in the old days." Bart chuckled, congratulating himself on figuring out the mystery of the blue eyed man, and rubbing the growing lump on the back of his skull where his head had smacked the sidewalk.

A Few Days Later...

ROOSEVELT SAT DRINKING malt liquor and playing solitaire at the poker table in the back room of the Burger Barn. He was waiting for the time to pass until he could open up his after-hour's club. Just as he pressed the can to his mouth, the door burst open and Bart charged in agitated and looking around fearfully. He was covered in spatters of blood, shaking and trying to catch his breath. The gray haired waitress, old Miss Raiford stood behind him in the doorway, terrified. Her hand covered her mouth, her glittering dark eyes wide, aghast at the bloody sight before her.

"Shall I call the police, boss?" she squeaked, staring first at Bart and then at Roosevelt.

"Not just yet Miss Raiford," Roosevelt said reassuringly. He motioned for her to quickly close the door as he pulled his .38 out and placed it on the table in front of him.

"It'll be okay, Miss Raiford, just get back to the restaurant. I can take care of Bart, here." Miss Raiford silently closed the door to the back room, leaving Bart and Roosevelt alone.

"Ya gots tuh help me, Mr. Rosevelt! I need a drink, bad. You got anything?"

"Here, take this."

Roosevelt pushed a bottle of Jack Daniels across the table toward Bart. He kept his eyes on Bart's hands the whole time, watching him intently. Bart grabbed the bottle with a bloody hand, looked at what liquid remained in the bottle and slugged it down.

"Man, what are you doin' bargin' in here like this? Are the cops after you Bartholomew?"

"Nobody saw me. I got way free as a bird. Cause I just kilt that fuckin' Mexican in St. Johns! Enrique I thinks they call him. Snuck up behind him as he got outta his car on Berkeley and shivved him, right there—got him in the back, good!" There was a predatory gleam in Bart's eyes. He was excited, triumphant and without remorse.

"Man you gotta get outa here! They gonna find you, Bart! You can't stay here, man. There's nothing I can do to help—nothin!"

"No! You gots tuh help me! You gots tuh! I need a place to lay low for a few days. I been snoopin' around St. Johns. They seen me, man! They seen me! They gonna figure out it was me!"

"Bart, you haven't been outa prison a month and already you's killin' people!"

"I hada do it, Mr. Rosevelt! I had tuh!"

"No, Bart. No one *has* to kill no one! You gotta leave!"

"I gots tuh—I gots tuh figur outa plan. Gots tuh get rid of them fuckin' Mexicans! Then I'll be back in business and Theda'll be ma woman again. Like how it used tuh be, Mr. Rosevelt! Just like how it used tuh be! I'll be in charge and they'll all be takin' orders from me! Just like back in the day!"

"Man, ya got blood on yo hands! Ya got splats on yo shoes and blood all over yo face! Oh jeez, man, I can't help you, none, Bart!"

"Ya gots tuh hep me, Mr. Rosevelt! Please?!"

"Bart, Enrique was prolly workin' with the cops, and if ya just kilt one of their own? I'm sorry man, but I'm too old to risk goin' back to jail! For you or anybody! Oh, Bart, you're just as crazy now as you was back then, and you ain't got no crew no mo!" Roosevelt fingered the .38 and tried to calm his rising fear. He took a deep breath and leveled his jaw, looking Bart in the eyes.

"Bart, you can wash up in the old sink over there and then ya gotta get. You gotta get outa here, quick! You understand me, boy?"

Bart looked at Roosevelt, a pleading expression on his face. He ignored Roosevelt's gun, he knew Roosevelt wouldn't use it on him. He was shaking less but still looked like a wide eyed frightened ghoul covered in blood. As Roosevelt watched Bart, he realized he was just an overgrown child doing the best he could. Despite the two men he'd killed in his life; he didn't have an evil nature. He just did what he thought he was supposed to do, even when it was the wrong thing.

"If ya wanna hide, Bart, you go downtown to skid row and get a bed at one of them shelters. Cops don't pay no mind to bums in line fer a bed. Mexicans won't look for ya there neether!" Bart hesitated, staring at Roosevelt's face hoping to see some compassion in his eyes, but Roosevelt wouldn't back down.

"Awww, come on Mr. Rosevelt? I thought you *liked* me?"

"I do like ya, Bart! And I liked your mama and your auntie too before they died, but there's nothin' I can do fer ya now, okay? This is bigger-n-you-n-me. I can't help ya, boy. I can't help ya if'n ya kilt somebody?!"

"Come on! I ain't got nobody! I'm all alone, now!"

"Man, didn't ya hear me? You-gotta-get-outa-here! The cops still come in here fer coffee ever damn night. Sometimes they knock on the back door here, to speak tuh me! Some cop is gonna walk in right behind you any second now wonderin' what the damn commotion is all about. Or the Mexicans! And goddamn it I don't wanna have to kill nobody!" Roosevelt fingered the .38 in his hand and waved it at Bart.

"I'm tellin' you to leave Bart! You can go and clean up. I'll let ya do *that,* but after that ya gotta take your crazy trouble witcha and get!"

"Yes sir, Mr. Rosevelt, yes sir!" Bart murmured quietly. "You was always respetful to ma mama so I'm gonna do as you say. I'm gonna be respetful to you just like mama woulda wanted—just like mama woulda wanted."

"That's right Bart, that's right."

Bart staggered to the old basin, an expression of hopeless despair in his troubled dark eyes. He bent over and leaned deep into the industrial sink, splashing water on his face and head. He soaped up with a fresh bar of Safeguard and rinsed off, cupping his hands together and brought the cold *Bull Run* water to his mouth again and again, drinking handfuls of the crystal clear, sweet water. He bent over the sink, resting his arms on it and was silent a long moment, still breathing hard. Without warning, Bart began to weep into the sink, choking, his shoulders shaking, sobbing outright—deep guttural sobs as the water fell from his face, soaking his shirt and neck, and the faucet continued to gush. Bart slowly turned the faucet off and it was suddenly quiet as he gulped air, trying to compose himself. They could both hear Miss Raiford as she swept the linoleum floor in the other room, muttering to herself and fretting.

"Oh, Mr. Rosevelt! Where did the time go? It went so fast, and I got nothing to show for it? I got nothin' to *show* for it. Gotta get back what I *had*. Gotta get my girl back! There ain't no other way. This the only way, the only way I know how tuh gets anythin' done!"

"And you get on some other clothes!" Roosevelt ordered, motioning Bart toward the back door, leading to the ally. He stood up and picked up an old brown coat on a supply table nearby and thrust it at Bart.

"Here! Take this coat and put it on, and you get somewhere and get yosef cleaned up proper. You used to know quite a few of the ladies, you just look one of em' up, okay?"

"You cayn't get in no shelter when ya been drinkin, man. I dunno what I'm gonna do! I cayn't stop drinkin'. It's the only thin' that keeps me..."

Bart's voice trailed off as the water continued to drip from his face and neck. He stepped out the back door, pulling on the coat and staggering down the rickety wood stairs into the cluttered alley behind the Burger Barn. He made his way past the discarded trash, broken bottles and rats scurrying amidst the ancient rose bushes, tall weeds, Daphné Amore, and overgrown shrubs. Bart turned back to Roosevelt, his eyes hopeful and boyish and still wet with tears.

"Thanks Mr. Rosevelt and I—I sho am sorry!"

"Sho thing, Bart, sho thing. You jus be careful now? You hear?"

"Yessir, Mr. Rosevelt, yessir!"

Miss Raiford timidly opened the back room door and walked into the room. She walked up behind Roosevelt as he stood watching Bart disappear into the Albina shadows. "He scared me to death, Mr. Roosevelt. I thought he was comin' after ya. I had this skillet ready to put upside his head if'n he tried anythin. But...oh, poor Bart. Oh that poor fool, Bart."

"Yes, Miss Raiford, that's right. That poor damn fool, Bart." They looked at each other shaking their heads but said nothing more.

Frank's Day Off

THERE WERE GENERALLY not many customers in the Lotus at ten in the morning. Frank slid quietly onto the end stool as Midge continued idly stacking shot glasses and trying to read the morning *Oregonian* at the same time. Frank said nothing, instead sorted through the mail he'd retrieved from his office and laid out enough twenty dollar bills to pay his rent for another month. Just then a transient walked in wanting to use the restroom and Midge finally noticed Frank, sitting there alone.

"Hey slick!" Midge said with a big smile.

"Good morning Midge."

"We heard you died and the pigs ate ya." Frank smiled as it had been a long time since he'd heard that one.

"Not dead yet honey." He looked up at Midge and thought she looked older than the last time he was in. The creases around her eyes seemed deeper, especially when she smiled and he thought her lipstick was too red, giving her a sad, desperate appearance. Frank nodded in the direction of the bum disappearing into the restroom with a curious look on his face.

"Him? They call him *Wing-nut*. He's just an old street drunk—he's harmless. The boss tells me not to let him use the john unless he buys something. But if I don't let him in to take a piss, he just pisses in the doorway anyway and then I gotta clean *that* mess up. Besides, he's not shootin' up in there, and he always leaves the john the same way as when he come in."

"Well there's that I suppose."

"Yep, that's right. So, what would you like to drink?"

"Just coffee, extra cream. No sugar."

"Since when did *you* start drinking coffee? Did you get religion from that woman you been hangin' with?"

"I never got religion and I'm not really hanging with her, its just business. Besides I've taken the day off. Lieutenant Hatch, my old police buddy from North is pickin' me up in a few minutes. We're gonna goof off and catch up on old times."

"He still at North? I thought he transferred downtown?"

"Oh yeah, but that was years ago. He's still downtown."

"I thought you said everybody at Headquarters *hated* you?"

"Not true. Hatch is a detective Lieutenant, now. We're friends from the old days."

"Correct me if I'm wrong but don't you always say you *have* no friends?"

"Well, there's Hatch, so I guess there's the one!" said Frank with a chuckle.

Midge placed the cup of hot coffee in front of Frank and set the powdered creamer next to it. Then she leaned over as far as possible to give Frank a view of her ample cleavage, spotted and freckled like a constellation of dark stars.

"Been missin' you around here, Frank. You should come round more often. I see you got the rent money for me, though. Thought you might be plannin' on movin' out soon. Thought ya might be givin' notice." A car horn honked outside signaling the arrival of Hatch.

"I dunno sveet haht!" Frank camped, trying to sound like James Cagney.

"I'll see ya ven I see ya." Frank gulped the rest of his coffee, sucked in some air to cool his tongue and waved at Midge turning to give her one last smile, as he eased off the seat. The horn honked again and Frank stepped out onto the sidewalk and into the blinding Portland sunlight.

Drinks and Conversation

THE MORNING SUN glinted off the gleaming Black '69 Cadillac idling at the curb. Beads of water ran down the shiny paint and dripped onto the street. Hatch rolled down the window and grinned at Frank.

"Let's go get drunk!" Hatch said. He reached over, and opened the passenger door. The leather seat was slightly wet and Frank wiped it off with his hand, as he slid into the front seat, leaning back.

"Just went through the car wash across the street from headquarters. The damned window wasn't rolled all the way up!" Hatch offered by way of explanation. He shoved a flask at Frank. "Black Velvet," he said. "Good Canadian. Sorry but I started without ya, man."

Frank took the flask, unscrewed the top and slugged down two big swallows. The whiskey cut through the morning coffee and hit the bottom of his stomach burning.

"That's pretty damned good," Frank said, coughing and wiping his mouth with the bar napkin he'd stuffed in his pocket.

"Good tuh see ya Hatch. Where we headin' buddie?

"I figured we'd hit Kelly's first, then later, we'll see!"

By the time Hatch and Frank drove the few blocks to Kelly's Olympian, Frank was beginning to relax. It was good to have a day away from the ghetto and the stress of being up all night and it was good to see an old cop buddy, too. He looked around the interior of the Cad and felt the leather upholstery, stroking it with his hands.

"This leather feels new, smells new too" Frank said, looking in the back seat.

"It is," Hatch replied.

"Damn, nice!"

"Yep, had it all redone. This '69 is a real beauty. I want it new inside and out. I don't care how much it might cost. Women like it too. I get a lot of thumbs up from the girls, and waves, when I'm out cruisin'."

"I see ya got a scanner. Jeeze, ya got a siren under the hood, too?"

"Nah, just a radio. Since I'm in charge of homicide, I need to know what's goin' on, even when I'm off work—like now. You know how it is."

"That, I do."

Hatch parked in front of Kelly's on Washington, checked to make sure the Cadillac was fully locked and headed straight for the front door. Frank followed him close behind, as Hatch headed to a far back booth across from the bar. Hatch waved to the bartender and seated himself with his back to the wall, facing out. Frank smiled at Hatch knowingly.

"Old habits are hard to break, huh Frank?"

"You bet, Hatch."

"Well, this *is* Kelly's you know. And you never know what's gonna happen. There's usually a cop in here though, drinkin' coffee if they're on duty and booze if they're off. You know the score."

"I sure do."

The bartender delivered a shot of Canadian Club and a beer back for Hatch and asked Frank what he wanted.

"It's been a while since I've had a Manhattan. That's what I'll have I think, and heavy on the sweet Vermouth." Frank fished for a cigarette in his pockets coming up empty except for his old Zippo.

"Damn, Theda musta smoked that last one."

"Sure miss havin' ya around, Frank. It's been a long time since we were both workin' the streets in St. Johns." Hatch leaned back, took a deep breath and rubbed his face.

"You remember when police work was *fun*, Frank? Back in the 60s—wrestlin' drunks and kickin' ass? Drivin' around with the siren blarin' and the red light flashing? We were the sheriff, then. We were in charge and there weren't so many fuckin' rules! People did what we said. Maybe it was just a small chunk of real estate, but we were the fuckin' *law!*"

"I remember those days, Hatch, when it was still new, when I felt like I was makin' a difference." Hatch sighed, looking past Frank as if searching for someone just behind him.

"A lot of the older guys are gone now. You're gone and— oh you remember Drake, right?"

"Oh yeah. Sure. He was kinda a prick as I recall."

"No shit. A couple years ago he got into an argument with a black guy on the mayor's staff and called him a nigger to his face. They had some history I hear. Rumor is the mayor's assistant was fuckin' Drake's ex-old lady. They got into a wrestlin' match right there in the mayor's office! I wasn't there, didn't see it but man, I sure wish I had. That woulda been great!"

"No shit, really? Damn. I'm glad I don't have to be around all the cheatin' and the lyin'. It's a got damn Peyton Place over there."

"Yep, well unfortunately for Drake there was an Oregonian reporter there waitin' on an appointment and he saw the whole damn thing. That little pencil pusher was more than happy to testify to what he'd seen. Drake was gone the next day. Locker cleaned out and desk drawers empty. His career toast and his pension burned, too!"

"That's tough. I can relate you know."

"Yeah, I guess you can. You know I tried to tell them not to go through with it, Frank. I put in a good word for you. Told em' they were wrong, told em' you were a damn good cop, but they wouldn't listen. They had it out for ya, why I don't know. Maybe cause you weren't dirty, but they sure had it out for ya, man."

"I know, Hatch. I heard how you went to bat for me. That's all ancient history, now."

"Anyhow, when Drake was workin' the street the NAACP was always tryin' to sue him for somethin! If it wasn't one thing it was another. Usually it was the shit he got into with the colored's in the North End. Knocking around all those young men, some of em just kids, you know? He hated the blacks, but he sure loved their dope. Shake downs is how he got in trouble with the NAACP, that and bein' too damn aggressive—too much of a hot dog. He got what was comin' to him. Drake always was outa control."

"I do seem to recall he was a showboat, and a prick. Always trying to screw some guys' girlfriend or wife. No respect for anyone, not even himself. He never bathed regular either. You remember that?"

"I heard the guys who went to academy with him nick-named him "Onion Shirt" cause he stunk. We got him straight though, just took a while—until he fucked up his entire career. He got shitcanned for more than just that situation with the mayor's assistant. It was dope; he was doing somethin' he shouldn't have been doing."

"Ah, the good old days, we did have fun Hatch, huh?" The bartender delivered Frank his Manhattan, sliding it over to him. Hatch scoffed, and smiled but said nothing as Frank laid out some money for a deck of smokes, sliding it over to the bartender.

"Marlboro's, the long ones if ya got em' please."

"Ya have to be a lot more careful whatchu say these days, Frank." Frank agreed, nodding his head and lowering his voice to match Hatch's confidential tone.

"You got that right—the wild sixties are a thing of the past."

"Who's this Theda you mentioned? Isn't she a black girl? "

"Someone I'm workin' for now. It was her brother, Jojo who was shot in the back over in the North End. They got a new one, too. Unidentified as of yet—the case O'Leary's workin' on? I'm just trying to locate a missing boy for his mother, and Theda, she's a friend of the family," Frank said quietly. "Or at least that's what she tells me. It's a job."

"You might as well forget that one old buddy. There's no evidence, no witnesses and between you and me, no real fuckin' interest. At least not from the dicks in homicide. This whole town is heroin heaven. That's never gonna go away."

"Well, at least *that* hasn't changed," Frank said, taking a sip of his Manhattan.

"It's gotten worse Frank. I don't know *who* I can trust anymore."

"Best not to trust anyone. That was always my motto back when I was workin' the streets. Didn't do me much good, though, did it?"

"O'Leary is probably the most honest dick in the office. Maybe he's gettin' his too but he thinks it was a theft or a robbery the kid was runnin' from when he got plugged. We erased it off the active board as a probable justifiable homicide after only a couple of days. I think the kid was number fifty five or fifty six this year. Everybody is getting killed these days."

"Is it really that bad, Hatch? Damn, what a number!"

"Oh yeah! And there was another murder just a few days ago. A Mexican named Longoria got stabbed and his throat cut. Right in front of his house on Berkeley. I think it was in the 7700 block. Bloody mess that was, blood everywhere." Hatch scratched his head looking past Frank, lost in thought and a million miles away.

"Yeah the 7700 block just off Lombard—anyway nobody saw nothin' and nobody heard nothin'. Funny how nobody ever sees or hears anything in the North End. Nobody wants to talk to the *po-lice!*" Hatch laughed bitterly at his own joke.

"*That* never changes," said Frank.

"Anyway, Longoria had a long record, mostly for dope."

"I remember the family; they were nothin' but trouble, even the girls." Hatch shrugged his shoulders. "Now there's one less of them, so we're not too upset over that one either. May that stupid motherfucker rest in peace. But can you believe the bad luck at getting' yer throat cut in front of yer own house?" Hatch shook his head, sipped his drink and chuckled.

"In front of his own house? Only in St. Johns I guess."

"Yep, Frank. *Only* in St. Johns!"

Both men sat in silence for several moments. They were remembering the old days, as they sipped their drinks, running one memory after another through their minds like the reel to an old black and white film. Frank opened his pack of cigarettes and lit one with the aging, falling apart Zippo. He pulled hard on the cigarette, tipping his chin up and blowing smoke toward the ceiling. Their mutual reverie was ended by the bartender. He stood over them with that universal expression on his face that said: *if you're going to sit here any longer you should order another drink.*

"Can I get you boys something *else*?" Hatch seemed irritated at the bartender's insistence. "Nah we're done here, son. Come on Frank lets go across the river to the Sandy Hut. Maybe we'll get a little more peace and quiet there." Hatch stood up groaning and hopping a little on his left knee, favoring his right leg and turning his head to scowl disapprovingly at the young bartender.

"You okay Hatch?"

"Oh, I'll live I guess. My right knee's never been the same since that one riot outside the Paragon summer of '68. That dumb drunken bastard. How could I have known the kid was an All Star wrestler? Oh well, he got his didn't he? We pig piled that stupid punk till he did the chicken and shit his pants."

"The good old days, huh?"

"The good old days, Frank."

Stepping out into the sunshine again, Hatch waved off the meter maid who was contemplating giving him a parking ticket. She didn't know he was a cop, till she saw him walking up. He walked to the car and unlocked it, looking over, smiling and saying hello.

"Frank, did that young bartender with his arms all tattooed and those tight jeans seem like a fag to you?"

"I wasn't payin' attention, why?"

"And what's with the ring in the nose thing?" Frank shrugged his shoulders, chuckling and didn't answer.

"Did you see all that metal that guy was wearin? There's enough metal there to hang a shower curtain!"

"Well, it is 1975, Hatch," Frank said.

"Remember vice in the early sixties, Frank? God, the harassment we gave those queers! I hated that job. Left as soon as I could. Nothin' but drunken cops who hated themselves and drove home lit every night."

"I didn't last long in vice either. I transferred back to the uniform after about a year. Drive on James!" said Frank, laughing. He slouched down into the leather seat, enjoying the warmth of the morning sun.

"Yes, to the Sandy Hut!"

"To the Sandy Hut!

More Conversation and Drinks

THE SANDY HUT, just south of Benson High School was a longtime watering hole for cops unwinding after work. The familiar feeling upon entering the dimly lighted bar came flooding back as Frank stepped over the threshold of the east entrance/exit. It brought back memories of after work commiseration—complaining about the stupid over educated cops who filled the ranks of the upper command structure and the frustrated street cops who had to do all the dirty work, while supporting wives and children.

Frank remembered one summer when he'd gotten some sun after a week off. He'd come into start shift and one of his buddies noticed his face had some color. "Hey, Frank! Did the Sandy Hut build a skylight? I notice ya got some sun!" That's how popular the place was with cops who came in to unwind after work, and if the cops were actually talking, instead of sullen and silent and brooding over their impossible professions, then it was usually a lively debate on how to get police work done and protect the regular citizen without coming under attack by the liberal media. The media was always willing to defend some bad guy at the expense of a good cop, but that was a national trend and most cops were used to it.

Portland was no different—like most of media Portland journalists would present some three time losing wife beater or child molester on the TV screen with the caption: "His mother said he was just turning his life around!" or "According to his live-in girlfriend, he was just going to start taking classes at the community college." That was always how it went…before the guy went for the cops' gun, or charged with an eight inch butcher knife, or tried to toss liquid oven cleaner on them.

"You know Frank, in a lot of ways you're better off than those of us still stuck in this job. Cause I gotta tell you, it's really killin' me." Hatch paused as the redheaded, big breasted waitress with the micro-mini and black fishnet hose served up a Manhattan with extra Vermouth and a CC with a short beer back.

"I mean you're a *free* man, Frank? You're your own boss, now. You're not tied up with these crooks anymore"

"I never thought about it that way, but yeah, I guess you're right." Hatch paused and both men watched the mini-skirt wiggle her way into the dim shadows behind the bar.

"You got out of this shit before you had to spend your whole fuckin' life at it just to get a little pension." Frank sighed and contemplated his old partner's words but said nothing.

"After ten or fifteen years it's not fun anymore, but then you already know that. The system gets to you; the bad guys just keep gettin' outta jail and come back at you. Then you wonder what the fuck cop work is about when the cops are the crooks half the time, anyway!" Hatch turned to face Frank.

"You know that's why they got rid of you doncha? You were too fuckin' honest, Frank!" Hatch turned to face the table and wiggled farther into the booth, leaning up against the wall.

"Assholes keep getting murdered. Robbers keep robbin', cars still get stolen, and kids keep stealing cigarettes and beer from the quick-sack stores. One day you come to work and see that stack of cases on your desk gettin' higher and higher and you jus' give up. You throw up yer hands and say fuck it. It ain't worth it. Fifty five fuckin' murders? In less than a year? It's unbelievable. And us cops are out riskin' our lives? For what? Can you tell me that? What are we risking our lives for?" Hatch emphasized his words by slapping the table top causing the redhead to look over with a frown, her ginger eyebrows knitted together in surprise and annoyance.

"For fuckin' what?" Hatch demanded, in a quieter tone. He turned and gazed at the redheaded waitress and smiled a charming *don't worry about it'* smile.

"I hear ya Hatch. I hear ya." Frank finished his drink and waved at the barmaid for another round.

"A little more on the sweet Vermouth this time, honey?" he asked as she strutted over.

"You know what Frank? It really boils down to just one thing. *Eatin'*. We all gotta have groceries in the fridge. We all gotta EAT! We gotta have a roof over our heads. We gotta pay the fuckin' bills. That's why us older guys hang onto a job that's drivin' us nuts—that's killin' us. Eatin! It's all about eatin! Fuck the citizens. Fuck the shady cops. Fuck this fucked up town. I want my *pension!*"

The alcohol was speeding Hatch's thinking along and the darkened but comfortable atmosphere seemed to be the right place to be for Frank.

"Maybe, I'm lucky, Hatch. Yer probly right. I don't miss bein' on the street even a little. It was such a damn hassle. And no matter what we did, it was never the right thing. Damned if ya do and damned if ya don't. That's the life of a cop. Just a hired gun workin' for cheap."

"Damn, if that ain't the truth. But you got out. I tell ya Frank, there are times I really envy you."

"Don't envy me Hatch. Look at me. What do I got in life? What do I got to show for all the work I done? Nothin, that's what! I got nothin!"

The west door of the Sandy Hut opened allowing a shaft of light to cut through the cigarette smoke and illuminate more customers arriving. They were three men; all off duty cops. They looked tired, but they had that swagger that only cops have when they're comfortable in their own skins—when they know they can fight, when they know they're strong and in charge. One or two of the faces were familiar and Frank nodded politely as Hatch waved in recognition, a tired smile on his face. The barmaid recognized the men and called out, "What'll it be guys? Yer usual?" The men waved and called out their favorite beer or whiskey drink. There was an urgency in their voices that Frank recognized. It said: *Hurry up! Shift is over and we're thirsty!*

"Ya know Frank," Hatch continued, "I get my pension in a little over a year now and ya know what I'm gonna do? I'm gonna take what's left of my cirrhotic liver and retire to the beach. I like the Tillamook area down there, maybe a little cabin at Bay Haven."

"I've been to Bay Haven. It's nice, little tiny place but nice."

"Yeah! I'm gonna fish. I'm gonna dig clams and be a regular at whatever local bar the real fishermen hang out at—and I'm gonna chase women, not like when I was a young cop. I'm really gonna put some thought into it!" he added as a serious afterthought.

"I'm gonna look for someone different, ya know? Young, fresh, don't drink or smoke. Pretty, and she's gonna have to have nice tits. That's gonna be a priority, Frank. Nice tits!"

"Let's drink to nice tits, Hatch!"

"You gotta girl now? Who's this Theda, again?" Frank took a deep breath contemplating his answer.

"Technically, she's my client. She and her…mother hired me to work a case. Wanted me to find an old boyfriend, and a brother who was missin' from NE. A skip trace. Pretty simple."

"Why were you askin' about that murder then, over on, where was it, Commercial?"

"Oh, I dunno, she thought maybe some other ex-boyfriend mighta done it. Didn't pan out though. I tried to find connections but there ain't none."

"Yep, it's a crazy city, Portland. Full of crazies and always will be."

"Crazy activist town, that's for sure." Frank didn't know what else to say so he left off there. "How about you Hatch? Do you have a little female flesh to come home to?"

"Nah. But I'm still lookin' I guess ya might say. Ya never stop lookin' do ya Frank? My ex-wives and I still talk, but that's about it. No sex anymore. No woman wants a worn out old copper with a bad liver who's been married five times."

"You know Midge, right? The day bartender at the Lotus. She's always lookin' Hatch. She's blond with big ones and a pretty good figure, too. And she's decent, you should look her up."

"What makes ya think I haven't tapped that, Frank?"

"Oh, I see! Well, okay then!"

Both men laughed heartily, finished their drinks, got up and left. The sun was still shining outside and the bright light dazzled their alcohol clouded eyes as they walked to the car.

"Guess we should go home," Hatch suggested, "While we're still upright." Frank agreed and slid into the comfortable leather seats of the Cadillac.

"The Lotus?" asked Hatch.

"Nah, take me to the Paramount apartments over there on North Broadway across from the Coliseum. You can drop me off there."

"Okay Frank. Hey, this has been fun, like old times. Sometimes ya just need to get drunk ya know?"

"Yeah, I'd say you're right about that, Hatch."

Hatch pulled in front of the Paramount Apartments and put the car in park. Frank opened the door, and stepped out, shaky on his feet. He turned around and waved as Hatch gripped the steering wheel. Hatch's mouth was loose and he offered a goofy smile, saying authoritatively, "Till next time, recruit!" Frank smiled and nodded, going along with the playful tone. He steadied himself on the sidewalk in front of the Paramount and watched as Hatch maneuvered the black Cadillac, swerving jerkily into the traffic lane towards the Broadway Bridge and then out of sight.

Frank fished in his pockets for the key Theda had given him and held onto the railing as he slowly negotiated his way up the worn marble stairs, carefully watching where he placed his feet. "I'm pretty drunk," Frank said to himself philosophically. "And it feels good. Tired of *playin'* drunk and not bein' drunk." He pushed open the front door and navigated his way along the worn hall carpet to the slow moving Otis elevator with the wire cage door, stepping inside. He pushed the third floor button, holding onto the rail to steady himself, and waited till the elevator came to an abrupt stop and creaked open.

Opening the apartment door with Theda's key, he stalked into the living room, clumsy and swaying on his feet. He stopped dead center in the middle of the room to dramatically proclaim "I'm drunk!" He stumbled over and collapsed onto the bed. Theda, who was reading a copy of *Vanity Fair Magazine* and enjoying a joint with her coffee, chuckled as Frank began to snore, softly. He was unconscious in less than a minute. Theda stood up, walked over and removed his shoes and .45 from the holster. She looked at the gun for a moment wondering what the stamped lettering "ACP .45" meant and stuffed it under the mattress where Frank usually stashed it.

She covered him with the patchwork quilt she had made by hand in Home Economics at Jefferson, tucking it into his neck and covering his feet and sat back on the couch and re-lit her joint. She gazed thoughtfully at Frank, realizing he too was vulnerable, a solitary person just like she was—just like a lot of people were. She felt a growing protectiveness. She wanted to brush the hair away from his forehead and stroke his brow. She wanted to touch Frank, to comfort him—but she didn't.

Bart Tries Again

FRANK AND THEDA had morphed into an unlikely nighttime team trying to catch Batman in the act. Frank knew he could trust Theda to stand her ground and felt confident she would use the .38 if she had to. They had become each other's back-up. Frank didn't worry as much about her being a block away anymore. As long as he could see her in the dim streetlight, he felt everything would be okay.

As another long night was turning into dawn, Theda signaled Frank it was time to go home. Batman wouldn't be caught this night, either. The long nights of surveillance was wearing on them, particularly Theda, but every time she thought of giving up, the picture of Jojo lying dead on the sidewalk beneath a drizzling Portland rain returned to haunt her. The mental image gave her new resolve. And for Frank it had ceased to become just another case. He and Theda had become close, closer than he ever imagined would happen. She was easy to be around, easy to talk to, easy to eat breakfast with. Frank would find Batman; then Jojo, Theda, and Roosevelt would have their justice. Besides, he knew after talking with Hatch, that if *he* didn't catch Batman, no one ever would.

Theda stood on the corner, feeling a slight chill as the wind drifted through her golden brown curls. Frank caught up with her but stopped suddenly. He turned his nose to the breeze, smelling the night air curiously.

"You smell that?" he asked.

"Yeah, I smell it" Theda said. "Kinda smoky, what is it?"

"Smells like Lips is workin' his Albina Barbecue," said Frank. Theda nodded, sniffing the breeze again, and shuddering at the possible origin of the offensive, half rotten smoky odor.

"Lips been around ever since I can remember," said Theda innocently.

"Since even *before* your time," Frank said with a dark chuckle.

"Is it true sometimes he…"

"Whatever your mama told you to keep you mindin' her don't think about it now. It's all lies anyway, honey."

"Wanna drink?" Theda offered the flask to Frank unscrewing the lid and extending it to him, her face expressionless.

"Whatcha got in there?"

"Some Mimosa."

"The girly stuff?" Frank asked. Theda gave him a look, and then smirked, laughing. Still, Frank took the flask and drank.

"Not bad tasting, though, when you get used to it."

"I'm a girl, Frank!"

"You're a girl, huh? Is that right?"

"Yeah, and I don't like the hard stuff! It burns goin' down."

"Yeah, well you get used to it in time!" Frank said. His statement seemed funny and he laughed, feeling bold enough to surreptitiously poke Theda in the short ribs when she looked away, surprising her. She jumped and squealed, putting her hands on her hips and grabbing the flask for another sip of Mimosa. She tried to poke him back but he danced out of her reach laughing.

"You better watch it, Theda!"

"Oh, really?" she asked as they strolled back to the car. By the time they drove back to Theda's apartment, the flask was empty and they were both giggling. The alcohol had gone to their heads. In their intoxicated brains, everything seemed funny and the world was a huge joke. Theda fumbled with the key opening the lobby door and *that* was funny. They had trouble opening the wire cage elevator door and *that* was funny. Theda stumbled on the jumbled hall carpet, and went careening through the air, arms flailing, legs akimbo, nearly falling and *that* was hilarious. They shushed each other, laughing and spitting, their eyes watering.

"We don't wanna wake up the neighbors, do we?" whispered Frank and *that* was funny.

"Whadda I care about the dang neighbors? They're all jerks anyways!" Theda said and *that* was funny.

As they took off their jackets and put the guns under the mattress, Theda began the nightly task of removing Frank's dark makeup. She began by wiping a clean streak on his forehead, and another down his right cheek with a wet washcloth. She poured liquid make-up remover onto her palm and smoothed it over his face, massaging it in. It was rich with mineral oil and soon dissolved the make-up. Stepping back she giggled at the oily mask on Frank's face, dark with streaks and smears. After another swipe or two crisscrossing his cheeks, he looked like a Maori warrior. Theda laughed and showed him his reflection in her compact.

"I like the look," Frank slurred, laughing.

"Oh, stop!"

"It makes me look fierce." Theda stood back gazing at Frank's face thoughtfully.

"Yeah, fierce! Bad-ass and—kinda sexy, too."

"Now, YOU stop. I'm an old man, honey."

"Oh, shut up. You're not an old man. You're just right, Frank. Just as you are."

"Is that right little girl?"

"Yes. It is!"

"10-4 good buddy!" Frank slurred.

"Oh, Frank!"

As Theda was wiping the last of the make up from Franks face, the mood changed with a sudden pounding at the apartment door. "It's me Bart! I need a place to hide out! Lemme in, Theda!" The words came through the door, loud and clear. "Lemme in!" Frank could see Theda stiffen. She clutched his forearm and held on, her eyes wide.

"Oh God Frank, he's gonna wake the whole place. We gotta get him outa here!"

"Lemme in Theda! Damn it, girl, I need some fuckin' help!" Bart was banging on the door trying to force it open with his shoulder. Theda brought her hands to her mouth, as her eyes began to tear up.

"He's gonna get me evicted Frank, just like before! Oh God!" Frank took her hand, tenderly.

"What do you want me to do, sweetheart?" he asked sobering up immediately.

"He's probably not gonna go away."

"Get rid of him! Please get rid of him!"

Frank walked to the door and opened it suddenly. This gave him the element of surprise as he stepped onto the threshold standing tall and looking Bart straight in the eyes. Bart looked back, startled. He stood shifting his weight from one foot to the other. Who was this man in Theda's apartment his eyes seemed to say. Frank rushed forward and slammed Bart hard on his chest, with open palms, causing him to fall back a few steps and stumble. Bart emitted a low growl and regained his balance, leaning forward.

Bart remembered Frank from his first visit to Theda's apartment and his eyes narrowed in recognition. Bart began to charge, as if to force his way in, but Frank gripped both sides of the door-frame and spread his legs wide. He was too large an obstacle and Bart couldn't force his way in. Frustrated, Bart yelled, "I need help Theda. The Mexicans are gonna kill me! Can't you help out an old beau? We used to love each other, remember?"

"Leave us alone, Bart! Get outta here!" Theda hissed, walking over to stand behind Frank.

"Awww, come on Theda!"

"Leave us alone! There's nothing I can do for you, anymore Bart!" Frank lurched forward, stepping over the threshold and shoved Bart hard on the chest again and into the hall. Bart went careening backward and landed flat on his back. As Bart was struggling to get up, he pulled a straight razor from his pant leg, brandishing it in his right hand menacingly.

Moving swiftly, Frank blocked Bart's right arm, and as he rose to his feet, Frank kneed Bart in the abdomen, thrusting his right knee square into the soft tissue of Bart's solar plexus, the area just below the sternum. Frank gripped Bart's right wrist, as the straight razor glittered, only inches from his face.

"If you don't stop coming at me with that fuckin' razor, I'm gonna use it to cut you up in pieces and throw the chunks off the fuckin' St. Johns bridge! You piss-complected puke. You'll be nothin' but fish food!"

Bart sucked air, and involuntarily dropped the razor to the floor. Frank reached down and quickly picked it up with his left hand, watching as Bart slowly fell back, collapsing to the hall floor and holding his middle, his mouth open and his eyes wide. Frank reached down and jerked Bart up by his shirt front, using only his right hand. Gripping the tattered shirt he spun Bart around and pushed him several feet to the fire exit door. Frank watched as Bart stumbled through the door and made his way down the iron stair, looking over his shoulder to make sure Frank wasn't coming after him.

As Frank stood looking down, his legs spread and breathing hard, he took the razor in his right hand and in one deft motion slammed it against the fire escape railing. It broke easily into two pieces, each fragment falling into the open dumpster three floors below. Theda hurried over to Frank, clutching his arm, and they watched as Bart disappeared, heading east, jogging towards the overpass, muttering and talking to himself.

"He reeked of alcohol and old sweat. Smells like he's been sleepin' in the fuckin' bushes," said Frank. Turning around, they entered the apartment door without speaking. Theda was holding onto Frank's arm.

"You went full animal on him, Frank. I didn't know you were so *strong!*" Frank looked down at Theda, and grinned, stopping and flexing his right bicep by way of response but said nothing. His adrenalin was pumping and he was still breathing hard.

"I can make us another Mimosa?" said Theda.

"Sure," Frank answered. "We could both use a drink. But the next time yer boyfriend comes at me with a straight razor?" Frank said, turning to look directly at Theda, "The next time I'm gonna *kill* him." Theda nodded saying nothing. She padded into the kitchen, returning a moment later with two water glasses half-full of the orange sparkling drink.

"Ya know Frank, he's *not* my boyfriend. That wasn't very nice. It's not like I've enjoyed any of this."

"I'm sorry honey, I'm just pissed off. I don't like getting physical like that." Frank fished around in his shirt pocket for a cigarette.

"I know. It's okay."

"It just came out. I didn't mean nothin' by it." He found a cigarette crumpled from his wrestling match with Bart. Pulling his Zippo out of his pants pocket, he gave it a flip. The top came off and skittered across the floor. He retrieved it and tried to put the two pieces back together, willing them together for just one last smoke.

"Fuck!" he said, "Fuckin' old thing." He stared at it letting out a heavy sigh. It had reached the end of its time with Frank. It wouldn't work anymore.

"I'll buy you a new lighter if that's what yer upset about?"

Nah," he said looking at Theda. "I kinda promised myself I'd quit when this old Zippo gave out on me. Piss poor time to quit on me though—when I'm stressed out like this." Theda set her drink on the coffee table and lit a joint.

"You know you don't *have* to quit just yet. You could smoke a few more days?"

"Nah, I promised myself I'd quit when this old Zippo gave up the ghost. And when you make a promise, you should keep it, especially when you make a promise to yourself."

"You should take a hit of *this!*" Theda suggested offering the joint to Frank.

"I don't know about that."

"It'll help your stress. You need to relax. Bart's gone, now." Frank contemplated the lit joint while also looking at Theda's pretty face. He reached for it haltingly, and then pulled back his hand.

"Oh, I dunno. The last time I smoked a joint was years ago when I was working vice. It didn't affect me. Besides it's illegal." Realizing how silly he sounded Frank laughed in spite of himself, shaking his head from side to side at the absurdity of it.

"This is quality product!" Theda said proudly. "I don't smoke shit. Take a hit with me—come on?" Frank looked at the deadbolt latch on the apartment door to make sure it was locked. He glanced furtively at the window and couldn't shake the feeling he was doing something wrong—something illegal that would land him in trouble. But he took the joint from Theda anyway, holding it like a regular cigarette. "Like this?" Frank asked, grinning and watching Theda's face intently, his eyes gently mocking her.

"No Frank! You know how tuh do it! Pinch it. Like this," she said repositioning the joint between his fingers.

"Pinch it? I can do that. I used to pinch lots of folks at one time," Frank said pulling on the marijuana cigarette.

"You're a regular comedian, Frank!"

Two Days Later...

AFTER GETTING OFF their shift Frank drank Theda's fresh dark roast coffee and ate orange marmalade on buttered toast. After breakfast, Frank drove to his office at the Lotus to pick up his mail and check phone messages, while Theda bussed over to the Burger Barn to check in with Roosevelt and pick up Frank's pay for the week.

Frank sat at the end stool waiting to get Midge's attention and sorted through the mail, putting his few bills in one stack and the requests from insurance companies in the other. He laid out his office rent money neatly on the bar as he usually did and waited for Midge to notice. After a couple of minutes it seemed Midge was deliberately ignoring him, so Frank walked to the end of the bar where she pretended to be reading the newspaper.

"Hey Sveet haht," he said trying his James Cagney voice again.

"How 'bout getting' Jimmy boy here a drink?"

"Oh you again? It must be rent time. You never come around now that you ran off with that black chick. She must be somethin' else!" Midge reached for the Vermouth bottle.

"I'll have one of those Mimosa things this time. They been tastin' pretty good lately." Midge shot Frank a look of disbelief, and laughed outright. She reached for a cold bottle of champagne and searched under the bar for a container of orange juice.

"Is that what sweetie drinks?"

Frank was beginning to enjoy the jealousy from Midge, it was endearing, but he didn't want to be unkind.

"It's just for a change of pace—and I could probably use the vitamin C."

"Lt. Hatch was in here, lookin' for you the other day. He left you a note he scribbled on a bar napkin. I *didn't* read it," Midge lied, smiling sweetly.

She handed Frank the note and the Mimosa at the same time. Frank gripped the cold glass in his hand and took a deep drink. He unfolded the napkin and read the message: *Frank, another nigger got his throat cut a couple nights ago. They found him at the cut, on the railroad tracks under Lombard Street out in St. Johns. I think you may remember him, his name was Bartholomew Williams. Another loser murdered in the North End. Can't stand it. Gotta get to the beach. Homicide number 59 this year."*

"Who's Bartholomew Williams?"

"I thought you said you didn't read it?"

"Sue me. What's this Williams guy to you?"

"He was a gangster of my acquaintance. Back when I was a cop and breaking my back for no one in particular."

"One of the gangsters you're workin' for?"

"No, this guy was a real gangster and not very smart. I kicked his ass a couple a times; back in the day and again just recently."

"Guess it's *your* business," said Midge as she casually walked away, trying to seem bored and picking up a shot glass to polish, but Frank could tell Midge was concerned, troubled.

"I don't mind talkin' Midge?"

"Lt Hatch wants me to go to the beach with him, if you can believe that?" Midge paused looking for Frank's reaction.

"You should go. Hatch is a good guy. He's lonesome, *and* divorced!"

"Yeah, well we messed around a while back, did a little dilly-dallying. He's an okay guy. I guess."

"Wasn't he married then?"

"So what if he was?"

"You should check him out, Midge. He's close to retirement and wants to live at the beach."

"The beach? Really?"

Frank leaned over and whispered confidentially: "And if you guys got married and he *died* you'd get his pension! Cause that's where he's headed, not the morgue but retirement. He's got another eighteen months to go, but if you two got married, you could get a job at the local bar if you wanted and dig clams on the weekends, make seafood stew."

"Seafood stew—oh boy!"

"Seafood stew is good Midge! They serve it at the Oyster Bar down the street."

"I prefer the salmon."

Midge stood up and wiped some drops of orange juice from the bar. She walked to the far end, staring at herself in the mirror behind the whiskey bottles. Maybe she would take another look at Hatch. He wasn't half bad in the sack—now that she remembered and she wasn't getting any younger. The wrinkles and heavy makeup reflected in the mirror gave her a moment's pause. Maybe she *had* been slinging booze at the Lotus a little too long. Maybe she *had* mopped up old Wing-Nuts piss in the doorway one too many times. Maybe it was time to say goodbye to Indian Charlie and George. Maybe it was time to dig clams at the Oregon coast with Hatch. And maybe her reflection in the mirror provided her with the right answer.

Shuffling Along Third Avenue

THE GREYHOUND BUS eased to a stop, parking in the downtown Portland bus depot north of Burnside. Charlie-Rides-The-Horse stood impatiently waiting for the driver to open the door, and still tired from his long hike to the bus stop earlier that morning. He had to catch the 8:05 A.M. bus and then take the long ride to Portland from Warm Springs.

The door opened as the air brakes let out a squawking hiss and Charlie set his sandaled feet onto the pavement. Besides his new brown leather sandals, he wore new grey sweat pants and his shirt pocket was full of money. The same length of rope secured his pants at the top and he carried a small cloth drawstring bag containing his gift for George.

Once in town, Charlie shuffled along SW Third Avenue, his bent figure in no particular hurry. It was not yet ten o'clock and George wouldn't be up and out of the basement just yet. Charlie passed the Maletis Grocery on third where he had purchased many *Mickey's of Tokay* back when he was younger. Only seventy five cents a bottle, and as many bottles as you wanted and nobody cared. The cops would pick you up if you passed out but you could always sleep it off in the drunk tank at Police Headquarters, down on Oak.

Crossing Third and Burnside Charlie passed a longtime burlesque theater, its glory days long over. The window in the ticket booth was smeared with oil and filth, and the doorway littered with cigarette butts, coupled with the rank stench of old urine. The sidewalk in front had a dirty sheen to it. It was caused from men shuffling their feet while waiting in line, spitting, smoking and drinking surreptitiously—their small silver flasks hidden in their coat pockets. Charlie wondered why white men stood in line to see naked women in a theater and after some thought surmised it just wasn't an *Indian* thing to want to look at something you couldn't have. No, that was a white thing.

Continuing south along Third Avenue Charlie stopped and looked up. He squinted at the fifth floor jail at Police Headquarters at Third and Oak. He couldn't see the bars but knew there were dozens of prisoners up there waiting for court or serving short sentences for the crime of being drunk in public. Charlie had spent many days and nights up there over the years, usually for being drunk, jay walking or begging. But after going through the system a few times the cops got to know Charlie and quickly made him a trustee if he had only a few days to serve.

Charlie did a good job of keeping the nap up by brushing the felt on the three pool tables in the officers' day room. He made a reputation for himself as being the best shoe shiner—shining officers' shoes before they went on shift. If another trustee already had the shoe shine job, Charlie would join the trustee crew in the basement of the garage and wash police cars. That's the way it usually went when Charlie came to Portland: party, get drunk, go to jail for a few days to sober up and then go back to the reservation for recuperation and maybe some of the gut-rot booze he could pilfer from a friend or two at the rez until his next check.

Charlie continued on his way toward the Lotus walking slowly and looking in store windows, killing time until he could see George. He stopped to look in the windows at the Portland Outdoor Store. They displayed Western shirts and Levi jeans and bright red western neck scarves, and boots. There were colorful horse blankets and decorated leather saddles and he wondered about the kind of person who came to downtown Portland to buy a saddle for a horse anyway.

The building was old and most of the paint was worn off. It looked tired and dirty from years of downtown dust, car exhaust and simple human waste.

The display window had a long crack going from the bottom all the way up to the top. It was held in place with silver duct tape. Charlie wondered if the story the old Indians at the reservation told was true; that when the Portland Outdoor Store was built, the street in front was dirt and the sidewalk made of wooden planks.

Looking at his reflection in the window, Charlie saw his own clothes, his shabby but comfortable Levi jacket, and his cleanest dirty shirt contrasted with the new grey sweat pants and new sandals. He saw an older Indian man with a long black braid and a starboard tilt to his stance. Staring for a moment more, he rubbed his finger over the crack, and decided the window would hold a while longer. He shrugged at his reflection and ambled down third with his head bent, looking thoughtfully at the sidewalk the whole time.

Charlie stopped to gaze in the window of the novelty store next. The windows were so dirty Charlie wondered when they'd last been cleaned. They sold whoopee cushions, rubber chickens, a marked deck of playing cards and brown plastic dog poop. He thought about buying the dog poop as a joke on George but decided against it. "Maybe next time I'll buy the poop and fool George," he muttered to himself. Turning away from the display window, Charlie continued walking and thought of the hot cup of coffee waiting at the Lotus. He kept a firm grip on the cloth bag that held George's gift, cradling it in his arms carefully, like a delicate baby animal.

Theda Gets the News

THEDA WAS IN the back room of the Burger Barn waiting to pick up Frank's pay and have lunch with her Grandfather, Roosevelt, but she was troubled.

"I need to talk with ya Grampa—about a few things I been thinkin' about."

"Well, you sit down here. I got sumpin' tuh tell you first, daughter. No way tuh say it but jus say it." Roosevelt took a deep breath and waited.

"Okay, Grampa, I'm listening?"

"Bart's dead, sugar. Your old Bart's dead." He paused, letting it sink in.

"Bart?"

"A railroad crew of Gandy Dancer's found him with his throat cut alongside the railroad tracks runnin' through the cut in St. Johns."

"The cut?"

Roosevelt nodded, and moved in his chair trying to get comfortable, his eyes never left Theda's face, as he searched her eyes for a reaction. She sat there, stunned and silent for a long moment.

"Oh, poor Bart!" Theda whispered softly, looking away.

"Looks like it was the Mexicans—cut his throat and dumped him off the Lombard Street Bridge. Must be 'bout 150 foot down to the tracks from the road." Theda looked down and studied her hands for a moment. She let out a weary quavering sigh.

"I turned him away, Grampa. When he was at my door beggin' tuh get in the other night. Frank was there and we made Bart leave. We told him to go."

"I feel bad too, girl. But he came in here only the other night. He was covered in blood and lookin' jus plain crazy. He said he killed Enrique jus a few minutes befo'. I had tuh turn him away, too. He was jus' too messed up tuh help. Had it in his mind if he kilt off his competition in St. Johns, he'd get his territory back."

"Why would he think that? Gone eight years and get his territory back, just like that?"

"I told him it was different now with the cops runnin' everything. He wouldn't listen, said he wanted you back. Kep talkin' bout getting' his Theda back."

"Never woulda got me back. Last time I saw him was before he went to prison for that long stretch. I'm sorry he's dead. God, poor Bart! That crazy fool—he was such a crazy fool, Grandpa!" Roosevelt brushed the faded green felt of the poker table with his hand trying to raise the felt nap covering the table.

"I know baby. I know." He smoothed the felt back and forth a few times, then pushed his chair back and sighed. "Killin' and robbin' and dopin' jus don't work no mo. Times is changed from them old days. Too many folks is involved." Roosevelt handed Theda the envelope with Frank's money for the week in fifty dollar bills.

"Thank you Grandpa."

"How's it goin' with the hunt for Batman?" he asked changing the subject.

"We're out every night," said Theda. She stopped to rub her hands together and look at her nails.

"Frank is determined, Grandpa."

"Good. Cause I got this picture in my mind of poor Jojo, layin' in the gutter gettin' rained on!"

"I know, Grandpa."

"Folks is upset and afraid with these murders. It's startin' tuh effect the after-hours business. Neon's, too."

"We'll get him grandpa. We will. Don't worry. We won't give up." Miss Raiford opened the door, peeking her head in and asked what they wanted for lunch.

"I'll just have some chicken in a basket. Thank you Miss Raiford." Theda said.

"And I'll have some fries smothered in gravy-n-cheese with chopped onions on top!" said Roosevelt with a grin.

"Mr. Roosevelt, you *knows* you ain't supposed tuh eat them greasy fries!" Miss Raiford scolded, grinning at him and shaking the big iron skillet she held in her hand, jokingly.

"Then shake the grease off and don't put so much gravy on. Need the cheese and onion though." Miss Raiford nodded and smiled.

"It'll be a few minutes," Miss Raidford murmured, quietly closing the door.

"That lil Miss Raiford! She always tryin' tuh look out fer me."

"Maybe ya should let her grandpa. You need lookin' after doncha?"

"Sometimes. Maybe, a little. She still comes by my place from time to time." A sly smile lit up his face and he seemed to be thinking of something else as he looked at the wall across the room.

"Grandpa? Grandpa pay attention, please?"

"Go ahead. I'm all ears."

"It's like this; when we catch Batman, *if* we catch Batman? I don't want Frank to go back to bein' a private detective workin' and sleepin in that junky old Lotus. I was thinkin' if I can talk him into it? Maybe-we-could-run-our-own-after-hours?! Make our money that way? What do ya think?"

"You sweet on him, aren't ya girl?" Roosevelt pushed back his chair and grinned at Theda.

"I do like him if that's what you mean!"

"You know he's a white man, Theda?"

"I know grandpa, but he's different. He's not like other white guys. He's not!"

"You sweet on him. I knows it and I bet *he* knows it, too."

"Oh, he does not, Grandpa."

"He's not some kinda kid Theda. He knows it. He hasta know, a man at least fifty. He ain't no spring chicken."

"Well, he ain't old neether, Grandpa! And yeah, sometimes I look at him and, you know…"

"Tuh be with someone different?"

"I guess, yeah."

"Them kinda relationships is fraught with trouble ya know?"

"Things is different today. Its 1975! And he's so cool about everything. He's calm and a gentleman and he looks after me! He does, he looks after me."

"I told this to Bart only the other day, and I'll tell you the same thing. Sometimes the right person come along. And sometimes the right person do the right thing. When that happens, the color of they skin and even a little age thing? It don't' matter. It don't make it *wrong*."

"He's a good man Grandpa. He stood up for me. There was a coupla times when Bart came around and Frank coulda jus thrown up his hands and say *this ain't my problem!* He coulda picked up his pay and never come round again. But he didn't run on me. He kicked ass for me. He kep me safe."

"Daughter, when you guys catch Batman, y'all can have *carty blanchey* out here as pretty as you please. There's a place I been lookin' at down on Mississippi where it cross with Shaver. Right behind the old Phipps Pharmacy on the corner. There's a alley behind the house too. Make it perfect for an after-hours place."

"Does it look good?"

"Its looks like it should be torn down—it's perfect!"

The door opened and Miss Raiford brought in their lunch pausing for a moment to make certain Roosevelt was pleased, as she stood with both plates in her arms. The sun was shining outside and it had infected Miss Raiford, giving her a jaunty step and a happy air about her as she placed both plates in front of Roosevelt and Theda.

"Thank you Miss Raiford," Roosevelt murmured.

"Thank you," said Theda sweetly."

"Of course," said Miss Raiford.

"Want me to stop by yer place later this evening Mr. Roosevelt?" she asked glancing down at him. Without waiting for an answer, she stopped to regally survey the room, smiling prettily and glided to the door, closing it behind her. Roosevelt looked after her sternly, then burst into a grin, glancing over at Theda.

"Don't you mind that. She's jus kiddin' there. Don't you make no never mind about that." Theda smiled knowingly and picked up half the burger, biting into it delicately.

Lips McGriffin's Crematorium

FRANK PULLED HIS Blue Charger to the curb on Williams Avenue and stopped alongside *Lips McGriffin Crematorium*. Getting out of the car he saw Lips and another man dressed in a black suit and wearing a chauffeur's cap. He watched them remove two large black plastic bags from the trunk of an early seventies dark colored Buick sedan and into a wheel barrow. There was just enough dusky morning light to see the shiny sedan had Idaho license plates. Frank waited until the car pulled out, driving north on Williams and disappeared on Killingsworth, speeding off, as Lips walked back inside, pushing the wheel barrow.

Frank walked down the newly vacated ramp to the basement crematorium, careful of his feet in the dim light. The stillness was unnerving. He tapped lightly on the overhead door. Frank saw two eyes peering at him through the small dirty window. They blinked in recognition and the dusty garage door rose slowly until it was high enough to duck under.

"Come on in, Frank. I heard ya wanted to talk to me."

"Thanks, Lips."

Lips motioned for Frank to enter and as Frank ducked in, he found himself in the common area of a spacious room. With a wave of his hand, Lips indicated Frank should sit and relax in a worn but comfortable overstuffed leather sofa. It was pulled up in front of two cremation ovens. The ovens had cooled enough to sit close by for the work Lips still had to do. The iron fire-proof doors were standing open to the ovens and the marks on the floor showed Frank that Lips had often moved the sofa back and forth over the years.

Frank sat down but felt uncomfortable in such macabre surroundings. To the right of the ovens were two gurneys. Each gurney contained the body of a dead man. Each man had traumatic injuries but the bodies were motionless and there was no blood. A severed arm lay awkwardly on one man's chest. On a gurney to the left of the ovens were the two black plastic bags. Frank had watched Lips haul in the bags only a few minutes before.

"So, what brings you around these parts, Frank?"

"First off let me say it's good to see you again. It's been too long, huh Lips? What brings me here? I thought you might have heard something about the four or five murders out here in the hood."

"I hear lotsa things, but ya know I don't know nothin'. That's my official position on things. Always has been, Frank."

"Of course it is. I was just hopin' maybe you'd heard something? Somethin' you could tell me?"

"Tell me what *you* know."

"Jojo, one of the kids murdered, he was Roosevelt's' grandson. You remember Roosevelt?"

"I do."

"He was shot three times in the back, robbed and left for dead in the street. Then a couple of nights ago an old gangster named Bart Williams had his throat cut and his body dumped on the railroad tracks out in St. Johns."

"Ain't none of the bodies came through here," Lips said shaking his head.

"Jojo's body has already been identified. Same with Black Bart, too. Both at the morgue. I'm just wondering if you'd heard anything about who the guy might be—the shooter?"

"I'm just dealin' with regular customers."

Lips pointed to the bodies on the gurney nonchalantly, then tested the heat of the open oven with his hand several inches away. With a small flat rake he reached inside and scraped out a small amount of brown sandy colored ashes, collecting them into a dirty plastic bucket with a wire handle partially wrapped in duct tape.

"Mary," Lips said, matter-of-factly, looking at Frank sitting uncomfortably on the couch watching.

"Who's Mary?" asked Frank. Lips reached in the oven again until all the ashes were scraped out and in the bucket.

"Who *was* Mary you mean?" corrected Lips.

"Yeah, who *was* Mary."

"That's her in the bucket. They said her name was Mary. Fat Mary—an old madam I think who drank her last glass of sherry. That's all there is of her—ashes. About six pounds," he said casually, showing the bucket to Frank. Frank wasn't sure what to expect. The bucket wasn't bloody and the ashes looked like regular ashes—like something you'd expect to find in the bottom of a backyard barbecue. Lips stepped in front of Frank and scraped the ashes out of the second oven into the same bucket.

"Jeeze," whispered Frank. "I never could get used to the autopsies and this is kinda the same thing. At least it feels the same."

"What's that? You spooked, Frank?" Lips laughed modestly, looking down as he continued to work.

"Don't you keep the ashes separate, Lips?"

"Not in *this* case," Lips answered.

"Why's that?"

"No one wants *these* two. Or the ashes of any of the ones you see here, now."

For a moment Frank was overcome and sat silent, brooding. He looked at the bodies on the gurneys and wondered what was in the two plastic bags. He was getting a bad feeling.

"Squeamish Frank?" asked Lips noticing Frank was silent and looking around the room uncomfortably.

"Well," Frank replied, and then he hesitated.

"Yes?"

"If I'da known you were working tonight, I'da slammed a couple of drinks, first. Yeah, I admit it, I'm squeamish. But I guess this don't bother you anymore."

"Been dealing with dead bodies all my life seems like, Frank. Joined the Army when I was a kid—they sent me to mortuary school before I went to work in what they call Graves Registration. I thought they assigned me a shitty job—for being black a-course. But it turned out to be a good trade. I learned the cremation business, and *now* it's hard to break into this business."

"You make pretty good money, huh Lips?"

"I got nothin' to complain about"

"That's good to hear."

"In the end, it's the best way to get rid of a body." Lips winked at Frank and stirred the ashes in the bucket with the metal rake.

"Looks like it."

"Not much left. They may come in here at 190 pounds but when I'm done with em' Frank, they come out ashes— six pounds, tops. That guy over there with the whacked off arm? He's small, maybe 150. He'll probably end up four pounds."

"What do you do with the left over ashes if nobody wants 'em?"

"They go into storage mostly. Sometimes I mix 'em in with the flower garden out back."

"How many you got mixed in the dirt out there, now?" Frank asked, apprehensive of the answer. Lips rubbed the grey stubble on his chin and thought for a moment.

"Maybe ten. Maybe sixty—seventy. Hard to say. Makes the flowers grow real good, though."

"I was hopin' you heard something about the killings?" Frank said steering the conversation away from cremation and the peculiar destinations of unlucky human remains.

"You know I hear lotsa things. Cayn't say what's true or not."

"You seem to have a lot of out of town connections," Frank said, pointing to the nearby bodies.

"All I can tell ya is what everyone else say. There's some guy out killin' folks."

"Maybe this Batman is from somewhere else," Frank mused, squirming on the couch to get more comfortable.

"Don't know. Wish I did."

"Yeah it's funny he's able to kill so many and no local rumble about who it is," said Frank.

"Any help from da cops?"

"No, Lips, no help. I already talked to them and they don't care. All the victims have been, you know..."

"Yeah, they niggas like me," said Lips chuckling softly. Frank nodded, looking even more uncomfortable glancing at the two black plastic bags on the gurney just a few feet away.

"You wanna drink a sumpin' Frank? You looks a little peak-ed. I know you ain't used to seein' this kinda stuff. At least for the last few years." Without waiting for an answer Lips poured a coffee cup half full of Hennessey's and handed it to Frank.

"Take the bottle too. I jus' took it outa the fridge, its ice cold. Have as much as you want, jus put it down on the floor by the couch when you had yer fill."

Frank took the cup and sipped it slowly, appreciating the burn and waiting for it to warm his insides and blank out the stress and apprehension. He poured himself a little more, leaving a sip in the bottle and set it carefully on the concrete floor. He drank slowly from the cup, feeling the relaxing effect of the alcohol, and leaned back on the sofa.

Glancing around again, almost furtively, Frank found a particularly comfortable spot lower down on the couch and stretched out his legs on it.

"You okay now?" asked Lips as he watched Frank closely.

"I'm alright, Lips, thanks."

"I forget this kinda stuff can be a shock to ordinary folk. Not many people come visit me down here. Too hot for 'em, you know?"

"I do," said Frank.

"I know ya seen lotsa dead bodies when you was a cop, Frank. The meat wagon'd come, bag the remains and drive off. You wrote the report and that was the end of it. What you see *here* is the other end of the process."

"Yeah, you're right about that."

"We unzip the bags and scoop out the remains. Whether they come down that ramp in a hearse or in plastic bags in the trunk of an old outa state car. It's all the same to me. They're fuckin' dead, Frank. If you talk to 'em they can't hear ya," he said raising his voice to make his point. "If ya poke 'em they can't feel it. And if ya cut 'em they don't bleed. They're just...I dunno, somethin'. Meat—not real now. They used to be somthin' but not anymore. Now they're just...inventory."

"Inventory."

"I get a thousand bucks a head for the legit ones and a grand and a half for the...the nameless ones. The Army did me a favor when they sent Private Lipmann NMI McGriffin to mortuary school."

"Ya got no middle name, Lips?"

"NMI, Frank. Not everyone does. No big deal."

Frank listened to Lips philosophy more comfortably because of the warmth in his belly and the supportive embrace of the sofa.

"Who are the two guys in the bags you brought in, Lips?"

"It's one guy. I *think* it's a guy, anyway. I'll know when I dump it out. He was too big to fit in the trunk in one piece." Lips noticed an uncomfortable look on Frank's face.

"I know what yer thinkin' but sometimes ya hafta make things fit. You can see how big the ovens are. If the inventory don't exactly fit, well—sometimes ya gotta shorten the legs, whack off the arms or halve em just to get em in the fire box." With Lips final description, Frank reached for the bottle, tipped it, drained it, wishing there was more.

"Then when I get the iron doors shut I turn on the gas and light the fire," Lips continued.

"Sounds like a lot of work and a lot of trouble."

"I gotta get the temperature up to the flash point as fast as possible. It takes some time depending on how big the body is. That's when the meat starts to cook and the fat starts to bubble and sizzle. We're all oil and fat, anyway. Did you know that Frank?"

"Well, I can't say as I did."

"Then the smell goes up the chimney—drifts all over sweet Portland," said Lips.

"That old Albina *Barbecue* smell," said Frank with a morbid grimace on his face.

"Yeah, that's what they call it. The Albina Barbecue!"

"The Albina Barbecue!"

"But as soon as the temperature gets up to about 2000 degrees? Poof! Everything in the oven just vaporize. The flesh is gone and the ashes are what you see in the bucket. It's simple physics. Everything will vaporize at the right temp-a-ture. Although before that, the head *does* explode."

As Frank contemplated exploding heads, and vaporizing flesh, the mental image of three .38 slugs hitting Jojo in the back in the same spot suddenly entered his mind. Simple physics; violent trauma and gravity. Destroy the spine, and the body collapses. Life is just physics, and in the end, so is death. The two men sat silent. The quiet was eventually broken by Lips, as he continued to think out loud.

"Look Frank, if I hear anythin' I'll get back to you, okay? When you get this Batman, though, you give *me* a call. I'll light him up for ya. No charge. A public service of Lips McGriffin, for the neighborhood. I *know* what he been doin' Frank."

"Thanks Lips. I appreciate that. Hopefully, I'll be callin' ya. If we're lucky."

"You can even come by the next day and scrape out the ashes if ya want. I'll put him out back by my potted Geraniums. We'll disappear this batman forever. Jus you-n-me."

"Thanks Lips."

"And for you Frank, I'd even do a pick-up. You jus' call old Lips."

The Conflicted Indian

THE DOOR OF the Lotus bar squeaked as Charlie-Rides-The-Horse pushed it open. Midge heard the door and poured a cup of black coffee for Charlie, as soon as she saw him limp in. He usually sat in an out of the way inconspicuous booth. And he usually complained about being interdicted, but now he sat on the end bar stool, placing his cloth sack on the stool next to him. He needed someone to talk to. He needed to talk to Midge.

"Why the long face Indian man?" asked Midge trying to cheer him.

"Uh, well sometimes hard to smile. Secrets...pain...here." Charlie thumped his chest, on the left, by his heart. "Here," he repeated, thumping his chest again.

"I'm...conflicted, I guess. Conflicted and interdicted!" Midge poured a cup of coffee for herself and leaned over the bar counter. She was interested in what Charlie had on his mind, as she was often interested in what people had on their minds and she was always willing to listen.

"I'm a traitor."

"That sounds pretty serious, Charlie. A traitor, really?"

"Uh...a traitor...yeah."

"Wow, are the cops lookin' for ya or sumthin'?"

"Not yet...but...maybe...if I tell, then my *people* will banish me." Charlie turned the coffee cup around in his hands before finally taking a sip.

"Traitor to white people too," he said looking up at Midge, with a worried glint in his dark eyes. Midge's expression changed from mild interest to apprehensive concern.

"Charlie, what the hell are you talking about?"

"Uh a murder. Been a secret. Well, maybe it was just a... death."

"You need to talk to someone right away, don't ya? This sounds scary. A murder, or a death?" Charlie picked up the cloth bag next to him. He turned it over in his hands several times then placed it carefully back on the stool.

"This is a present for George," he said pointing at the bag.

"A present? That's awful nice of you, Charlie."

"I give it to him. I bet he's awake now." Charlie got up, placed the bag over his shoulder and headed for the door.

"But what..." Midge started to ask.

"Uh, I drink on it more. Maybe talk then."

You Don't Spit Into the Wind,
and You Don't Mess Around With...

FRANK SAT ON the end stool, once again getting comfortable in the Lotus. He began the morning with a tall Bloody Mary as he fidgeted with the celery stick. He held it in his mouth, crunching it and drawing circles on the varnished bar with the wet swizzle stick. He pushed his mail out of range of any water droplets and began staring at the surface of the polished counter.

In the shiny surface Frank saw Theda's large golden eyes and without consciously being aware of it, he could smell her perfume, *Tabu*. He realized part of what he had been feeling was jealousy whenever Bart was around Theda. Now, Bart was dead and Frank wondered how things would work out. How would Theda react when she learned her old lover had been murdered? Theda intruded upon Frank's thoughts and it was difficult to push her out of his mind.

It wasn't just that Theda was beautiful; she was also decent, vivacious, intelligent and full of life. The more Frank thought about Theda, the more he realized he *didn't* want to push her out of his mind. Sitting at the bar, he focused on how the celery crunched one small snap at a time when he bit into it slowly and evenly. He wondered why celery complemented tomato juice and Vodka. Who thought up these drinks? Was there some science behind it? Is that why they were so habit forming?

A part of Frank—a part he didn't care to admit—felt sorry for Bart and people like Bart. He felt sorry for him because he was ghetto-stupid and because Frank knew Bart probably hadn't been given many breaks or opportunities in life. Part of Frank figured if Bart hadn't *been* so ghetto-stupid he wouldn't have tried to murder his way to the top, targeting the St. Johns dope business to do it. It was after all, 1975 and things were changing. The sixties were long gone in Albina and St. Johns. It was a new world.

Frank suspected, it was probably the Mexicans who dealt Bart his final blow, but it would be a while, before he knew for sure, and he knew the police wouldn't care. So much for Bart's trouble, Frank mused. He wound up dead, like so many before him. All his ambitions and desires dead with him on the railroad tracks in a crappy part of town, in a pool of blood. Hatch would be tearing out what was left of his hair with this new one, and it would go unsolved, tucked into the Cold Case File like all the others. Hatch needed to solve some murders and was beginning to show the pressure of an impossible job; that job was police work and Frank was sad for his old friend.

Frank also felt incredibly tired. He sat leaning over the bar with a blank expression on his face. He was trying to summon up the energy to face another day when a gradual dimness manifested to his right. Someone was there, standing in the doorway, but he didn't know who. He began to turn slowly at the growing presence.

"Frank McAllister? I'm here—and I'm gonna—I'm gonna 'rest ya fer murder!"

Frank turned quickly to look at the person standing in the doorway and saw a disheveled, unsteady and very drunk Detective Cunningham struggling to stay upright. His shirt tail was pulled out on one side with the other side barely concealing the snub nosed .38 stuffed snugly behind his belt. His mottled pink and blue necktie hung loose at the throat and one of his black wingtips was untied, with the laces trailing dangerously close to the toe of his other shoe.

"McAllister? You're under arrest—you stupid fucker—for the murder of—of Bart Williams!" Cunningham slurred, taking a step forward.

Frank sat on the stool, facing Cunningham and watching his every move intently. He unbuttoned his jacket to better handy up his 1911. He could see Cunningham was armed and *could* be dangerous, but he was just a bit off his game because of how drunk he was. In fact, Cunningham was way off his game.

Midge scurried quickly to the far end of the bar, getting away from whatever was about to happen. Four or five other early morning bloody Mary drinkers also carefully eased themselves off their stools. They moved toward the restrooms, past the bar and into the darkened back room, walking sideways with widened eyes. Cunningham continued to sway, pausing to steady himself before lurching forward, in his effort to get closer to Frank. Several more steps brought Cunningham near the end of the bar where he held onto the corner with one hand. He stood not quite in breathing distance from Frank, glowering.

"You murdered Bart Williams and you're under arrest McAllister, you no-good..." Frank turned his head to escape the alcohol fumes drifting from Cunningham's offensive mouth. Then he turned back and looked Cunningham straight in the eyes, his chin level, his demeanor confident.

"How did he die?" Frank asked matter of factly.

"You know damned well how he died! You stabbed him in the back and cut his throat, like some kind of fuckin' animal! Then you tossed him over the overpass. He fell at least a hundred feet to the railroad tracks, where most of his bones were broke!"

"Not my MO," said Frank, calmly. "*If* I were ever to kill anyone. Cutting someone's throat is too personal, too messy. I'da shot the guy and left him leaning against the railing. You got the wrong man, Cunningham. Go home and sober up."

"Not so fast McAllister! I'm followin' up on leads. Motive McAllister. *You* got motive!" Frank could see Cunningham was caught up in some kind of paranoid delusion. It was obvious, as an investigator that Cunningham was also trying to save his own ass. They needed to get some murders solved. All the guys in homicide needed to—before the mayor or citizen activists started complaining about a disengaged police force that just didn't care about the little people.

"What's *my* motive, officer?"

"Officer shit! I'm a detective, you fucker!"

"Some detective, yeah!" Frank smirked, giving Cunningham the once over.

"You killed him so you could have that sweet bit of brown sugar! She's mighty fine, isn't she? You like em young doncha? Hatch told me he dropped you off over at that nig's apartment. I'm thinkin' you're likin' that black stuff, huh Frank? How about it Frankie? You eliminated your competition. Ya don't have Hatch to stick up for ya so let's have the truth. Come on, out with it!"

Cunningham let go of the bar where he had been steadying himself to reach for his handcuffs. In the process, his feet got tangled up and he fell to the floor with a loud thud, landing painfully on his muscular back, his legs and arms comically askew.

Frank watched the slow motion adagio of Cunningham as he fell backwards, falling so hard he had to suck air before he could speak again. He saw Cunningham reach for the .38 in his waist band, as he lay on the floor. Before he could get it, Frank moved, fast. He jumped off the bar stool, landing on his feet with his knees bent and his legs spread. He pulled out his .45 and pointed it straight at Cunningham, right between the eyes.

"If you wanna die drunk, stupid, and on the floor of the fuckin' Lotus, then you just keep reaching for that belly gun, and you'll have your wish. Cause when I pull the trigger on this piece here, you'll be one damn ugly mess to clean up. Midge might hafta call the fire department to spray your stinkin' remains out into the gutter on Third. Out in the gutter—where ya belong!"

"McAllister? You're gonna…"

"Turn over, get up and get the hell outa here! I don't ever wanna see yer ugly face again, Cunningham, unless it's on the slab at the morgue—you big stupid gorilla!" Cunningham turned over, brought his legs to his belly and lurched to his feet. He staggered to the door.

"This ain't over McAllister!" he shouted over his shoulder.

"Oh, yes it is. It's over, now get outa here!"

Cunningham looked like any sulky drunk being thrown out of a bar as he stumbled though the threshold turned right and disappeared down the street. Frank walked to the bar and laid a five-spot down to pay for his drink and ran his hand through his hair. "Christ!" he muttered.

"Was that drunk guy a *real* cop?" asked the thin voice of a young woman. She was in the back of the restaurant, where the patrons had taken refuge.

"Nah, just a drunk lookin' for a place to piss. It's all over now. There's nothing more to see here, folks. Carry on." Frank paused at the door, looking in both directions up and down the street, to make sure Cunningham hadn't returned, waiting to ambush him.

"What just happened?" asked another voice from the back, this time from a feeble old man. As Frank walked outside, getting ready to meet Theda and running his hands through his hair again, Midge answered the old man. "I'm not exactly sure. But I think someone just tried to pull the mask off the Lone Ranger."

The Proposition

FRANK TOSSED HIS overcoat on the couch and lay down full length on Theda's bed. He kicked off his shoes and stuffed his .45 under the mattress. His legs were tired from standing out in the night and he sighed deeply wiggling into the comfort of the clean bedding.

"Ya know, I forgot to tell you cause it was kinda a funny thing, but when I went to pick up my mail at the Lotus yesterday I almost got arrested! For killin' Bart!

"What? Are you serious?"

"Yeah, that stupid Cunningham, drunk off his ass mind you, so fuckin' drunk he could barely stand, staggered in when I was sittin' there drinking a Bloody Mary. Said I was his "number one" suspect! Said I had the motive. Said I killed him so's I could have *you* all to myself."

"Well, you're not the first man to want me."

"Come on, I'm serious. He *really* thought that. Then he tried to throw down on me. Couldn't believe it! I beat him to the draw, of course—sent him on his merry way with his tail between his legs. The stupid fucker thought he could arrest me on a humbug. What a load of horse shit!" Theda felt comfortable enough with Frank to slip off her jeans and lay beside him. She propped herself up on one elbow—the lace of her red panties just visible from beneath the pullover shirt that covered most of her slender hips.

"Well, did ya? Did ya kill Bart so's you could have me all to yourself?" Theda pouted playfully, and fluttered her eyelashes as Frank watched her, a faint smile forming slowly on his mouth.

"I thought about it. Wondered if you'd be worth killing for."

"Oh really?"

Frank and Theda stared at each other for along moment. Then they looked elsewhere, possessed of a sudden shyness.

"Frank?" Theda said, trying to change the subject, a feminine lilt in her voice. She touched his shoulder demanding his attention.

"Yeah?"

"I've been thinking."

"Oh boy. Well, let's hear it."

"You know, I think we need to go into business *together!*"

"Okay, slow down now, Theda."

"We could run our own after-hours club, Frank! It could be as nice as you want. Fancy or not. *Frank's Place* we could call it, or *Theda's Place* or *Frank and Theda's Place.* The OG's are willing to help! I already talked to my Grandpa about it and the others. They willing to help Frank!"

"I don't know. I know you mean well, honey, but I just need to be on my own."

"Listen Frank, you're cool with them for stickin' with the job. For not givin' up on us. All we have to do is make sure we get our cut of the poker tables, sell good whiskey and have a little pot. We can be our own bosses! It'd be good!"

"Why are you thinking along these lines? Why now?"

'I don't want you goin' back to your detective job. Sleepin' in that dusty little office of yours downtown? On a couch? That's no way to live, Frank?"

"I'm doing okay, my needs are simple."

"Oh, come on Frank? Will you at least think about it?"

The tone in Theda's voice and the sincere look in her youthful and suddenly very innocent eyes told Frank he would have to come up with the right answer. He sat up, swinging his long legs onto the floor. He sat at the edge of the bed and turning his head, he studied the curve of Theda's hip, as if he was trying to memorize it, his eyes flicking up and down her body brazenly.

"Whatcha lookin' at Frank?" Theda asked.

"I'll think about it," Frank said, ignoring her question. Finally, his eyes traveled from Theda's body to her liquid amber eyes with a tired longing he struggled to hide, just as the dim morning light drifted into the apartment, pushing away the night. "I'll think about it," Frank repeated. He stood wearily, walked to the couch and lay down, draping his arm over his eyes, and thought about it.

Indians Don't Have Round Metal Hoops

CHARLIE-RIDES-THE-HORSE EMPTIED HIS wad of money from the pockets of his sweat pants. He laid the bills out in a crumpled pile on top of the worn plank bar. When his pockets were empty and the bar was covered with cash he sat back in one of the rickety chairs. He leaned over the bar and smiled at George sitting in his wheel chair.

"Here's the *smile money* Officer Arnie needs. You don't hafta worry 'bout this month."

"Charlie, you don't gotta do this?" George was surprised and a little overwhelmed by the generous gesture. "For real Charlie; you don't gotta do this."

"Oh yes I do!" said Charlie, his voice raised slightly and was more forceful than he intended. Charlie sat back in his chair, and looked down at his hands, calming down from his sudden outburst. He turned his face away as a tear formed in the corner of his eye. He opened the cloth bag and carefully removed a dream catcher, his gift for George, made with his own hands.

It was a y-shaped branch from a scrub pine tree with the bark whittled off. Between the two small limbs Charlie wove a web of thin cut deer hide. Hanging from the web were two Magpie tail feathers, about eight inches long one white, one black. Interwoven were three small smooth stones Charlie gathered from the Warm Springs River. Tied at the top of the web was a small piece of Calico fabric now faded but once perhaps pink and green. Charlie looked at it and handed it carefully to George.

"Uh, I made it. Dream catcher. For you."

"It's beautiful Charlie. I've never seen anything like it. They sell dream catchers down at the Saturday market by the river. But they're round with lots of colored feathers."

"Ha!" said Charlie in contempt. "Indians never have round metal hoops! From nature we make our own objects. Besides, Saturday market? Them jerks, they use chicken feathers!" The door at the top of the stairs opened and a piercing shaft of sunlight illuminated the narrow stairway.

"It's just me," said officer Arnie picking his way carefully holding onto the wooden handrail. As he approached the bar he shared his recent news.

"Got some terrible news for you guys. Just got the final divorce papers from my lawyer. My wife got the house and about a third of my monthly pension. That miserable, bitch!" Arnie sat down on the closest chair while George poured him a full shot glass of Old Crow and opened a Millers, sliding it over to him.

"This is terrible, do you know that?" demanded Arnie, waving the letter. He took off his police cap, adjusted his gun belt and stretched out his legs.

"My feet are killin' me already and the day is just gettin' started. I got thirty days to move out of the house and find me another place to live or I'll be homeless. Who woulda thought! Man, this is *just* my luck!" Arnie kicked off his shoes, bent over and began to rub his tired old feet. Charlie smiled at the thought of officer Arnie being homeless, but he still couldn't picture Arnie sleeping under the Morrison Street Bridge, or napping on a park bench. So, he continued twirling the dream catcher, touching it and blowing gently on the feathers to make them turn.

"And the worst of it is I'll have to work a few more years to pay into the system more, and make my pension better. I won't have any feet left, by then!" he moaned.

"Can you get a desk job?" George wondered out loud.

"Boring! Sitting answering stupid questions all day. And there's *no* smile money when you work the desk." Charlie motioned for Arnie to scoop up the money laid out on the bar.

"I pay for this month. It's all there. You can count it." George opened his mouth to object to Charlie paying the entire amount, but Charlie held up his hand.

"No! I do it now." Arnie smiled, stood up and began collecting the money, and smoothing it out in nice flat piles before folding the cash neatly in his wallet.

"I'll count it later. I know you wouldn't stiff me. It might affect my memory, in the long run. But I know you wouldn't stiff old Arnie." He grinned, looking at both George and Charlie gratefully, and held out the empty shot glass for a refill.

"There ya go Arnie,"

"I'm sorry it's gotta be this way boys, but this is how it's always been."

"We understand Arnie," George said kindly.

"I need to rest for a bit. The crooks can wait. I'm gonna go over there and lay back in that nice old overstuffed chair ya got there, George and rest my eyes for a bit." George smiled and waved his arm in the direction of the old soft chair, as Arnie shuffled over to the chair and fell into it heavily.

"Any time Arnie, any time!" George said with a good natured smile in his voice. He opened a beer for himself and poured Charlie a shot of whiskey and the three men sat drinking in silence.

"You know when this job was fun?" asked Arnie, rubbing his ankle and shoving his wallet deeply into his jacket pocket, a quizzical look on his face.

"You remember right, George? I was the taxi cab inspector and I had that little hole in the wall office at Central Precinct?"

"Of course, I remember, Arnie. You took our pictures, but that *was* a long time ago."

"I issued all the cabby's licenses and took their pictures. It was great." Arnie paused to finish the shot of whiskey and held out the glass for one more, as George wheeled over to the end of the bar.

"I remember I got a cut of all their side action and that's where we first met. You were drivin' Radio Cab #7 at night and makin' bucks, remember?"

"Yeah, you were taxing me pretty heavy then, too," George said, then flashed a friendly frown at Arnie.

"A coupla' fifths a week plus cash. But it was okay. We made it Alice and me. We were livin' at the Hamilton. She was workin' as a maid there and I was drivin' cab at night." George moved forward in his wheel chair and waved his beer at Arnie.

"Hey, you remember when the American Legion National convention hit this town a few years back?"

"Boy, do I ever!" replied Arnie rubbing his ankles again. My feet remember it, too. It was the summer of '70. Twenty five thousand Legionnaires hittin' this town all at once for a full week. My post was at Broadway and Salmon. Parade duty every day in the summer heat. Sweat running down my neck and all for some meager overtime pay."

"I kept three cases of whiskey in the trunk of the cab and sold out every night. $20 bucks a fifth, take it or leave it. I was runnin' so fast I couldn't stop to get gas. Delivering girls to guys at the big hotels—The Benson, The Marriott and the Hilton and takin' guys to girls, too. I didn't have time to sleep. But I was making the money!"

"Did I get a cut of all that?" asked Arnie laughing.

"Sure, every dime I made, and a few bottles of hooch to boot!" said George. He grinned back at Arnie. "It was fun while it lasted."

"I remember that time, too," said Charlie.

"Do ya Charlie?" asked George.

"The merchants hired security guards to make all us unde-sirables leave town. A few of us were Warm Springs Indians and we were escorted to the bus depot as pretty as you please. They gave us a bus ticket and made us leave, just like that. Guess company was coming to town and they didn't want us drunk Indians around. We was just part of the unwanted debris. They swept the streets and that meant getting' rid of me and mine."

"I kinda remember that part too, Charlie. We had a lot of people in the drunk tank who weren't really drunk. They were there jus to clean up the streets," said Arnie philosophically.

"Uh, George—how'd you meet your missus?" asked Charlie changing the subject. George poured Charlie another shot of whiskey and sat back in his wheel chair to offer up his remembrance.

"Why do you wanna know Charlie?" asked George.

"Oh, I dunno, I jus like to hear a good story, I guess."

"Let's see, I was first in line at the hack stand down at the train station waitin' for a fare. She was just sitting there in one of her pretty little dresses, lookin' so sad and so cute. "No place to go and no money to get there," she said when I asked her if she needed a ride. It was between train arrivals and no one was lookin' for a cab. We chatted a bit longer. I thought she was awful cute, short brown hair, chubby face, too much pink lipstick, but it looked good on her, with her bright green eyes, yeah, it looked real good on her. We wound up riding around. I turned off the "for hire" sign and we talked. Took me a while to get her to open up and then she told me a little bit about what she was up against."

"What was her story, George?" asked Charlie.

"After an hour or so of drivin' around, I took her to my room at the Hamilton. I could tell, she was lost, running away from something she didn't want to talk about. From Minnesota I think. Her old man run off with another woman.

We kinda felt safe together, ya know what I mean? We clicked right off. Meeting that funny woman was the best day of my life and probably the worst day for her. I think back now, and I realize if she hadn't met me that day, she wouldn't have been killed out here on the corner by that crazy drunk."

"Yeah, I remember that day George. Sad day indeed," said Arnie.

"The traffic cop said the car careened on down the sidewalk, took out two parking meters and the old police call box that used to be there. Disappeared down the street, never seen again. My Alice was dead and my legs wouldn't move no more." George lowered his face and tried to hold back the tears welling in his eyes.

"All I remember was it was a sedan, goin' fast, brown as I recall, or maybe gold."

Charlie touched the piece of tattered cotton cloth fashioned into the dream catcher and watched it twirl as he blew gently on it. His eyes teared up and he turned his face away, rubbing his eyes as if he was tired. There were more drinks served and reminiscing before the three succumbed to the alcohol and dozed off. Snoring could be heard in the Blind Pig as Charlie lay over the bar, his head resting on his arms, and Arnie lay back in the overstuffed chair and George slept in his wheel chair, his head drooped over his chest. Officer Arnie would do no police work and he would miss his free lunch at Dinty's.

Do the Right Thing

FRANK PUSHED THE door open to his room at the Lotus. It resisted, squeaking loudly. He turned to look at Theda standing behind him with her purse dangling from her hand.

"Open it!" she said, pushing on the door herself, impatiently. The door opened a bit more, but it was made difficult by a large pile of mail and magazines which had gone through the mail slot and landed in a pile on the floor.

"Lord!" said Frank holding his hand over his nose as they walked into the stale room, the dust motes swirling in the dim light. They bent over and began picking up the mail and tossing it on the desk. Frank headed for the couch and sat down heavily, while Theda walked to the desk and sorted through the mail, handing Frank a few important looking letters. He opened a couple of envelopes, reading slowly.

"The bank guys are mad at me," he said looking up at Theda. "I haven't been keeping up on the cars they want repo'ed."

"You don't have to do that no more, Frank." Theda tossed another advertising flier on the floor and stared at him with some impatience.

"You haven't slept here in ages, honey?" The word *honey* sounded right coming out of her mouth, and Frank glanced over and smiled at Theda. He stood up, and bundled the mail under his arm, opening his file cabinet. He pulled out several file folders and stuffed them under his arm.

"Yeah, it's not the same here anymore," Frank said. He looked around his small office wiping at the dust on his desk and looking at his fingers in bland disgust.

"Let's go see Midge and pay this week's rent, anyway."

"Yeah, let's go see old *nosy* boobs!" Theda gave Frank a sardonic smirk.

"I got the rent money right here in my purse." She stuck out her chest and stood tall, lifting her chin and smiling. Frank motioned for her to go first and they walked out of room ten, and closed the door behind them. Theda hoped it would be the last time they ever left that sad, dusty little room.

Midge looked up as they entered the bar and sat on the stools near the end. She watched as Theda opened her purse and carefully laid out the rent money, just as Frank had always done before. Frank waited until Theda was done setting the money down before stacking up some of his files and his mail.

"You guys movin' out of your office? Ya haven't been there much anyway." Midge looked pointedly at Theda and then at Frank.

"Not just yet, Midge."

"What'll ya have, Frank?"

"I'll have a bloody Mary please and the young lady here will have a Mimosa." Midge waved at an annoying fly that kept dive bombing her.

"Sure, coming right up, Frank" she trilled with false sweetness. Midge walked to the end of the bar for clean glasses and returned a couple of minutes later with both drinks in her hands. She looked over at Theda with a disapproving expression.

"You know Frank, Hatch and I are an item, now!" Midge said as she slid the drinks across the counter.

"Come again?" said Frank, an expression of interest and surprise on his face.

"Yeah we probably won't be around here much longer. He's gonna retire down by Tillamook, maybe get a little cabin at Bay Haven. Hatch seems to like Bay Haven. We're gonna fish—we're gonna dig clams, and we're gonna be a regulars at whatever local bar the real fishermen hang out at. That's how Hatch put it."

"Midge, that's wonderful! I think you're doing the right thing. Hatch is good people."

"Won't be for a while though, he's still gotta pull his pin."

Frank looked around at the old bar room and shook his head. He glanced at Theda and noticed she was smiling. Theda knew what Midge was doing and it amused her.

"Midge, you can't stay in this dump forever. Besides the Lotus will be torn down eventually—unless some rich guy saves it, for posterity, but that's unlikely. You know how the city leaders in Portland are. They don't give a damn about old buildings with ghosts; don't matter to them if they're built like a fortress."

"Oh yes! The basement ghost. I swear it's true. But you're right Frank. The entire tenderloin is disappearing. Just plain disappearing. I was afraid I'd disappear with it. But it's true— Hatch *is* good people. Just took me a few years to realize it." Midge leaned over the bar with the towel in her hand and pointed to a back booth where Charlie-Rides-The-Horse was quietly grieving into his cup of coffee, his voice thick with sorrow, as he murmured and whispered.

"Frank, this old Indian's been tryin' to tell me somethin'. Somethin' terrible. Somethin' about bein' a traitor—about a murder. He needs to talk to you. He's *interdicted* you know, but I'm feeling so sorry for him I put a little whiskey in his coffee." Theda looked over at Charlie leaning his head over the table and moaning softly.

"Frank, we should see what's going on with him. He seems so...miserable!" Theda said softly. Midge nodded her head eagerly in agreement. Frank shrugged his shoulders, and looked back at Theda.

"Can't you see how busy we are?" Frank asked in quiet consternation.

"Frank, it would only take a minute. You used to be a cop, right? What can it hurt?"

"Midge, I'm not a cop anymore. Can't he talk to Hatch, or somthing? Why's he gotta talk to me? Hatch works homicide. I'm a nobody now, just a licensed PI with no clout. Besides I'm up to my ears in dead people at the moment—figuratively speaking." Theda scooted off the bar stool and walked over to Charlie sitting in the booth. She reached over and touched him lightly on the shoulder. When he looked up, Theda could see the tears in Charlie's velvety brown eyes. She turned back to Frank and Midge at the bar.

"Frank? We need to help this poor fella," Theda called over.

"At least…listen to him?" Midge whispered. Frank shook his head no, his mouth a tight line.

"Charlie can talk to Hatch about a murder. This is not my job, anymore. Finish your Mimosa and let's get outta here," Frank called over to Theda.

"No! You need to listen to him, Frank!"

Theda walked back to Frank, her heels clicking on the tiled floor and placed her hand on his arm. She looked him in the face, her eyes pleading. Remembering what Roosevelt told her she repeated the words giving her version her own interpretation.

"Sometimes the right person comes along. And sometimes that person will do the right thing, Frank. You might be that person he needs right now. You need to at least talk to the poor man. It's the *right* thing to do. He needs to feel someone will at least *listen*!" Midge poured another shot of whiskey for Charlie nodding her head in agreement and walked over to the booth.

"Theda's right, Frank," Midge said firmly as she looked back at Frank still on his stool.

"Why are you two girls gangin' up on me? What's the deal?"

Frank stood up from the bar stool with a deep sigh of reluctance and walked to where Charlie sat, scooting into the seat across from Charlie, but not sure of what to say or how to begin. The two men stared at each other, Charlie with a forlorn look on his face, and Frank with a disgusted and angry expression, each waiting for the other to speak.

"Uh, I see you sometimes in the hall upstairs," said Charlie hesitantly.

"I have a small office. Room number ten, it's on the south side."

"Yeah, I know. I live in Warm Springs most of the time. When I come to town I stay here. Room eighteen. Close to bathroom." Frank nodded, the look on his face softening.

"Midge says you used to be a cop."

"I'm not a cop anymore..." His voice trailed off as he waited for Charlie to get to the point. Midge knew if the liquor dicks walked in she would lose her servers license for giving whiskey to an interdicted person; especially an interdicted Indian like Charlie, straight from Warm Springs.

Charlie held the shot glass up that Midge had given him with both hands and looked at it as a ray of sunlight penetrated the glass, giving it a warm amber appearance. He held it like that for a moment, and then brought it to his nose to smell it as if it possessed some unseen magical properties. He swirled the liquid in the glass and then swallowed it in one gulp. Charlie set his jaw and exhaled the fumes through clenched teeth, slamming the empty glass down on the table to punctuate the moment. Then he placed his hand over his heart in a dramatic display of emotion that under any other circumstances would have made Frank laugh out loud.

"Pain here. Much pain. Much sorrow. I speak now." Frank looked down and sighed, disgusted.

"Okay, we're here to listen," said Midge.

"Uh, my cousin, Tommy-Builds-The-Fire? Long time ago he run over and killed...Alice, George's wife. George's fine woman, Alice. The car paralyze George. No one knows, but now I must tell. My heart can't carry this heavy burden no more. Tommy-Builds-The-Fire is dead now, too. So much pain caused from this stuff we drink. So much pain"

"Go on," Frank said tiredly.

"Tommy got lotsa money from Timber shares. He come to Portland. Bought new Green and gold Cadillac from dealer on 12th street across from Benson school. Paid cash. Drove off. Tommy-Builds-The-Fire drank much whiskey that day. Drunk, jus blind drunk."

Midge twisted the bar towel around her wrist nervously, dismay showing on her face. Theda nudged Frank and gave him an *I told you so* look as she scooted in, sitting next to him in the booth. Charlie paused to wipe his mouth and blow his nose with the paper table napkin. He looked at Theda for encouragement.

"Go on Charlie. We're here for you," Theda said, "We're listening."

"Tommy-Builds-The-Fire plowed through the crosswalk here on Third Street. Hit parking meters-n-old call box on corner. Remember that old call box, Mr. Frank?"

"I sure do. Had to use it more than a few times as I recall."

"He drive back to reservation. Over grass and down into ravine near our shack. I find him next day asleep in front seat. Engine ran until outa gas. Cadillac smashed in front. Pieces of parking meter stuck in grill. Blood, too. And one small piece of...one small bit of cloth stuck in broken headlight. Pink and green, calico." Frank sat back in the booth and looked up at Midge.

"Guess you should get us another drink," Frank said with a resigned look on his face.

"Sure thing, Frank!" Midge said, walking back to the bar.

"We might be here awhile, yet." Frank sighed and placed both elbows on the table waiting for Charlie to continue.

"Go on Charlie. Finish your story."

"Tommy-Builds-The-Fire never left the rez after that. He never left again. He was like...haunted, like haunted man."

"Nobody said anything?" asked Frank.

"No, you know how it is. Our silence protects us, as best it can."

"That was three years ago, now, is that correct?"

"Yes, but it was secret. It was secret!"

"A woman was killed, though," Frank said firmly. He couldn't hide the exasperation in his voice.

"No one said anything? Why?" Frank asked.

"Well? Uh? She was...she was white woman. We always taught not to care—to hate. To hate hard—white people." Midge had returned to the booth and set down two more drinks. She couldn't disguise her disappointment.

"It wasn't important because she was a *white* woman?!" Midge asked aggressively, sneering. Charlie stopped talking for a moment to consider Midge's question.

"My ancestors camped here. Right here!" Charlie used the empty shot glass again for punctuation, slapping it down on the counter.

"And?" Midge challenged.

"The river is near. Smoke from our fires cured the Salmon caught from the river. Then the white men come. Now Indians pushed over one hundred miles back to mountains. Now there are parking meters. Cross walks. Cars. Indians didn't have cross walks or cars. We walked free, or on our horses! Our whole way of life, poof. Just taken away." Midge looked sadly from Frank to Theda. They were all thinking the same thing, realizing that what Charlie had said was true.

"The Cadillac is still there," Charlie continued.

"Cash receipt in jockey box. Six thousand dollars and four cents. 121.7 miles on odometer. At first, I think Tommy-Builds-The-Fire hit a deer, but no parking meters on highway. No, couldn't be that."

"But Charlie--a woman was killed?!" said Theda, touching Charlie on the shoulder. Charlie sighed and laid his large brown hands over his face.

"I come to Portland always," Charlie continued, letting his hands fall, in exhaustion into his lap. "I usually find good enough drink here. Then I meet George at Blind Pig. We drink together. Become friends." Charlie covered his face again with his hands, speaking through his long, thin fingers.

"In time, I figured it was Tommy-Builds-The-Fire who ran em' down...in his drunkenness. Three years—three years I watched rain drip off bent door molding and run down cracks in the broken glass. Three years—I watched heat waves shimmer off crashed metal. Car sits rusting and broken. Like George. So, I try tuh help George. You know? I buy him breakfast, I bring cash. Pay Officer Arnie's smile money for George. Bring presents made from my heart!" Charlie pounded his chest in emphasis, finally dropping his head. Frank began to say something, but Charlie held up both hands, asking for silence.

"More to tell. I make dream catcher for George. Make from tree branch near my shack. Magpie feathers hang down, I find in the meadow. Smooth stones from river and small bit of cloth caught in broken glass of car? Alice's dress, I think. George, he don't know. I don't say. Don't know what to do now? How do I make this heavy feeling go away? How do I make this right?"

No one spoke for awhile, not even Frank. They were all affected by the emotion of Charlie's story, each wondering what to say, each touched by his sincere tone and sorrowful manner. Theda touched Charlie's arm and looked at him until Charlie met her gaze.

"Charlie? Please don't tell George—or anyone else. It wasn't your fault. This is the kind of secret you have to keep. Do you know what I mean? The kind of secret you have to hold close to your heart and never let go. It *is* a burden but it's also a gift, too."

"Alice must know how sad I feel? She must know how much I didn't want dis tuh happen?" Charlie mused into his coffee cup.

"That's right, Charlie! And you're George's friend, now. It would be unkind to tell him the truth. Keep this secret close to your heart. And *be* his good friend and that will be all that this world requires of you!" said Theda.

"I don't gotta tell?"

"No, Charlie. You don't."

Charlie looked up at Theda and his eyes glistened with pooling tears. He smiled a crooked smile and reached up holding out his hand. Theda accepted his hand and Charlie took her hand squeezing it tightly. He brought Theda's hand to his cheek as two tears made their way down his face, and his eyes closed tightly, a quiet sob escaping his throat. Frank swished the last of his drink in the glass and swallowed it touching his empty glass to Charlie's empty shot glass as it rested on the table. The two men looked at each other, their eyes clear with a deep understanding neither man would forget.

"Theda's right. Mum's the word. This is the kind of secret you can never tell anyone, Charlie," Frank said, his voice just above a whisper. "This secret is as precious as a diamond. You have to be its keeper and protect it and never let it go."

Paladin, Paladin, Where Is Your Home?

FRANK WAS RIGHT about the law of averages. It always came down to just that—the law of averages. He had his costume down pat that final night. Theda did up his dark makeup just right, and his stagger-stumble was perfect in every sway and nuance. Frank looked like the kind of victim Batman would be searching for as he loitered near Roosevelt's after-hours club, stumbling back and forth, and pretending to look for someone near the alley leading to Roosevelt's back door. Theda was just down the block, watching and nervously fingering the .38 in her coat pocket. She had an unencumbered view of Frank as he played his part stumbling down the street, pretending to be drunk, pretending to be that new made to order victim.

Batman parked at the curb two blocks away on North Commercial. He was watching people leave the after-hours club, and waiting for the right victim to arrive at just the right moment. Feeling confident Batman started his muffled engine and pulled away from the curb, with the car barely moving forward down the street and not making a sound.

Batman would take the old drunk wearing the long overcoat that seemed lost—the tall thin man in his early fifties. He looked lean and well-built, but he seemed easy to take, he didn't look strong enough to fight. The black '69 Cadillac coasted down the street, and came to a stop near the thin old black man, bent over and muttering. Batman opened the passenger door, and leaned forward.

"Gimme yer money you stupid fuckin' nignog!"

Frank spun around and looked at the vehicle to the side of him. His mind raced. One thought after another now rushed through his consciousness. This *wasn't* Hatch's Cadillac! There *was* no leather upholstery! But the blue steel revolver pointed at his guts *was* a police .38 special! There was no denying what his eyes were telling him.

"A good three shot grouping," Hatch had said. Then it hit Frank.

Batman was a cop!

"Sure, sure, jus' a minute..." Frank mumbled.

He lurched toward the open car door, reaching in his coat, as if for his wallet. Faster than he thought possible Batman saw a .45 and felt the blow of the slug tearing into his chest. The impact of the slug slammed him against the car door and threw his head back hard enough to crack the driver's door window into a wide spider web pattern of shattered glass. The sound of the .45 going off rocketed down the street like a sonic boom reverberating off the darkened houses and old buildings, slowly dissipating, and echoing into the cold Albina night.

But which cop was *this* guy? Hatch? Drake? It didn't matter now. Frank had already passed sentence when he pulled the trigger. He knew the man would die. He walked over to the car, reached in and grabbed the black ski mask, gripping it in his fist and pulled it off in one deft motion. Frank was stunned when he saw the dying man across from him.

"*Cunningham?!*

"Fuck off, McAlister!"

"You worthless shit! What are you doin' out here robbin' and killin' people? For what? For what? I shudda known it was you. Man, I shudda killed you at the Lotus, when I had the chance. I shoulda killed ya, then!"

Frothy blood erupted from Cunningham's mouth, traveling down into the folds of his neck. The blood was scarlet and filled with oxygen—as scarlet as a scarlet rose. Cunningham sucked in his last breath.

"Them nignogs killed my Angie. They murdered my...I was getting revenge. Only what them animals deserve! I was getting revenge—revenge!"

As the words left Cunningham's mouth, his eyes became dim and unfocused and his throat rattled with the grotesque gurgle people make when they draw their last breath. Cunningham's eyes stared past Frank into the night sky, and whatever light in them was extinguished like the slow exhalation of a breath.

Frank looked both ways, up and down the street to make sure he was alone. He felt a chill wind ruffle his hair as he reached in and picked the spent cartridge up off the carpeted car floor. He reached down and turned off the police scanner and the ignition. Careful to leave everything as it was, he eased the car door closed with his elbow. He noticed blood splatters on his gloved gun hand, just as he heard Theda running up behind him, her high heels slapping against the icy cold pavement. She'd heard the gun shot and before he knew it, she was right behind him tugging at his coat, desperately, like a small child needing attention.

"What happened? I heard the gun. What're we gonna do?"

"I got the guy who killed Jojo," Frank said in a terse whisper, breathing heavily.

"Really? Who was it?"

"Nobody important. Just some guy."

"But who? Who was it?"

"Like I said—nobody important. Just a crook from the old days when I was wearin' the uniform. Just some guy I shouda killed, then."

"But what's gonna happen? What're we gonna do?"

"Nothin' baby. Nothin's gonna happen. We're just gonna walk away."

Theda froze and looked up at Frank. Her eyes were soft, and she seemed confused and pleased at the same time. Her parted mouth was glossy as she looked up at Frank with wide eyes.

"Did you just call me *baby*, Frank?"

Frank didn't answer. He looked down at Theda, a small smile forming. His blue eyes glittered as he opened his long coat and pulled her inside. The silver curls over his forehead began drifting in the rising wind as he wrapped his arm around Theda, pulling her in even closer.

"You did, didn't you? You called me *baby*?"

"Shhhh," Frank whispered to Theda.

Walking together under his long black trench coat, Frank and Theda turned the corner, still clinging to each other and hurried into the inky darkness. They stepped over broken concrete, empty beer cans, shards of glass and overgrown dandelions. The yellow light from the old street lamp, faint on their disappearing backs followed them as they made their way along the darkened Albina Street.

"Where'd ya park the car, baby? I gotta call Lips. He needs to make a pickup."

THE END

Appreciation

THANKS GO TO my good friend Phil Stanford, author of *Portland Confidential* and *Rose City Vice*, for egging me on to continue writing, for reading this manuscript in its many incarnations, as well as providing useful feedback, thoughtful critique, an excellent blurb, and for his valued friendship over the many years.

Thanks go to my good friend J.D. Chandler, author of *Hidden History of Portland Oregon,* and *Murder and Scandal in Prohibition Portland,* for his friendship, his lively encouragement to continue writing and for reading my manuscripts, offering good ideas for change, and pushing me to write "longer" which is a challenge for me. Thanks to J.D. for being the best Portland historian archiving unusual Portland crime data and sharing that knowledge with us all.

Thanks go to Doug Crispin for his support and for giving me a voice to share my working history as a Portland police detective at events that he has hosted. And thanks for being an ace Portland historian who values our history.

Thanks go to J.B. Fisher for his friendship and support and for being part of our gang of crime interested authors who are dedicated to researching, writing about and laying down the facts and the theories of crimes which sometimes remain unsolved. And thanks to J.B. for the excellent blurb he wrote in support of my book.

Thanks go to Olivia Croom for her book design and her cover design, which was exactly what I wanted. Thanks to Olivia for her patience in working with us over more than one galley edit and in creating the beautiful cover.

Thanks go to Bruce Broussard, newspaper publisher, businessman and television personality for his support of my writing, and for promoting my first book *Behind the Badge in River City: A Portland Police Memoir* on his cable access television program *Oregon Voter Digest*. Thanks to Bruce for adding to the reality of the dialogue in the book with the borrowed usage of his expression, "It's all about eatin!" And thanks to Bruce for his good friendship over the many years since I was first on his program in 2006, when I ran for Multnomah County Sheriff.

Thanks go to Fred Stewart, longtime Portland real estate broker, aspiring politician and well-known and well-loved local Portland personality, thinker and communicator. Fred is also an historian of some note, with more inside information on longtime north and northeast Portland families than anyone I know. Thanks to Fred for his friendship and for his unwavering encouragement of me, in writing down the history and stories of Portland, in both memoir and fiction.

Thanks go to Sheila Ahern, cherished family friend who has extended her faithful and loyal support and encouragement to my wife and me for many years. For all that you've done, Sheila, words cannot express our joint gratitude to you.

Lastly, thanks go to my wonderful Theresa, who is my wife, my best friend and a cranky editor. I thank Theresa as co-conspirator in all things that pertain to writing, for it is she who has made this all possible.

About the Author

Photo by Wes and Dot Weber, on the steps of the Lotus Hotel, 2014

Don DuPay was born in Wenatchee, Washington, where he spent most of his childhood, later moving to rural Montana for a short time while his parents bought and then sold a farm. He settled in Portland Oregon permanently in 1947 at the age of eleven. DuPay graduated from Grant High school in 1954, and then studied for two years at Lewis and Clark College. He went on to spend three years active service duty in the US Navy performing top secret radio surveillance on the Baltic Sea, rising to the rank of Cryptographic Technician T-branch E-6. After completing military service DuPay joined the Portland Police Bureau in 1961 where he sought to "make the world a better place by putting bad guys in jail." He rose to the rank of detective on 1967, and was eventually promoted to homicide detective. DuPay worked for PPB until 1978 when he resigned under doctors' orders and for documented medical reasons, which included severe depression and a serious bleeding ulcer. He became the director of security for the Benson Hotel for several years during the 1980's, and was instrumental in changing hotel safety policies that would ensure better safety for customers and for the actual building with regard to fire code violations. He later volunteered as co-host of a cable access television program called *Cannabis Common Sense* for almost five years. In 2017, DuPay graduated from Portland State University with liberal arts degrees. He was honored in the commencement program for being the oldest graduate of that year. Don DuPay resides in Portland with his fourth wife, author, poet and editor Theresa Griffin Kennedy who is also a native Portlander. He continues to write and be published.